www.EffortlessMath.com

... So Much More Online!

✓ FREE Math lessons

✓ More Math learning books!

✓ Mathematics Worksheets

✓ Online Math Tutors

Need a PDF version of this book?

Send email to: Info@EffortlessMath.com

TASC Math Prep 2020

A Comprehensive Review and Step-By-Step Guide to Preparing for the TASC Math Test

By

Reza Nazari & Ava Ross

All inquiries should be addressed to:

info@effortlessMath.com

www.EffortlessMath.com

ISBN–13: 978-1-64612-142-7

ISBN–10: 1-64612-142-2

Published by: Effortless Math Education

www.EffortlessMath.com

Description

TASC Math Prep 2020, which reflects the 2020 TASC test guidelines, provides students with the confidence and math skills they need to ace the TASC Math test. This comprehensive Prep book with hundreds of examples, over 2,500 sample questions, and two full length TASC Math tests is all you will ever need to fully prepare for the TASC Math. It will help you hone your math skills, overcome your exam anxiety, and boost your confidence -- and do your best to succeed on the TASC Math Test.

Whether you are intimidated by math, or even if you were the first to raise your hand in the Math classes, this book can help you incorporate the most effective method and the right strategies to prepare for the TASC Math test successfully. *TASC Math Prep 2020* is a breakthrough in Math learning — offering a winning formula and the most powerful methods for learning basic Math topics confidently.

The surest way to succeed on TASC Math Test is with intensive practice in every math topic tested--and that's what you will get in *TASC Math Prep 2020*. Each chapter of this focused format has a comprehensive review created by Test Prep experts that goes into detail to cover all of the content likely to appear on the TASC Math test. Not only does this all-inclusive workbook offer everything you will ever need to conquer TASC Math test, it also contains two full-length and realistic TASC Math tests that reflect the format and question types on the TASC to help you check your exam-readiness and identify where you need more practice.

Inside the pages of this comprehensive prep book, students can learn math topics in a structured manner with a complete study program to help them understand essential math skills. It also has many exciting features, including:

- Content 100% aligned with the 2020 TASC test
- Written by TASC Math tutors and test experts
- Complete coverage of all TASC Math concepts and topics which you will be tested
- Step-by-step guide for all TASC Math topics
- Over 2,500 additional TASC math practice questions in both multiple-choice and grid-in formats with answers grouped by topic, so you can focus on your weak areas
- Abundant Math skill building exercises to help test-takers approach different question types that might be unfamiliar to them
- 2 full-length practice tests (featuring new question types) with detailed answers

TASC Math Prep 2020 is the only book you'll ever need to master Basic Math topics! It can be used as a self–study course – you do not need to work with a Math tutor. (It can also be used with a Math tutor)

Ideal for self-study as well as for classroom usage.

About the Author

Reza Nazari is the author of more than 100 Math learning books including:
– **Math and Critical Thinking Challenges:** For the Middle and High School Student
– **GRE Math in 30 Days**
– **ASVAB Math Workbook 2018 - 2019**
– **Effortless Math Education Workbooks**
– **and many more Mathematics books …**

Reza is also an experienced Math instructor and a test–prep expert who has been tutoring students since 2008. Reza is the founder of Effortless Math Education, a tutoring company that has helped many students raise their standardized test scores—and attend the colleges of their dreams. Reza provides an individualized custom learning plan and the personalized attention that makes a difference in how students view math.

You can contact Reza via email at:
reza@EffortlessMath.com

Find Reza's professional profile at:
goo.gl/zoC9rJ

Contents

Chapter 1:
Whole Numbers

Math Topics that you'll learn Chapter:

- ✓ Rounding
- ✓ Whole Number Addition and Subtraction
- ✓ Whole Number Multiplication and Division
- ✓ Rounding and Estimates

"If people do not believe that mathematics is simple, it is only because they do not realize how complicated life is."
— *John von Neumann*

Rounding

Step-by-step guide:

Rounding is putting a number up or down to the nearest whole number or the nearest hundred, etc.

- ✓ *First, find the place value you'll round to.*
- ✓ *Find the digit to the right of the place value you're rounding to. If it is 5 or bigger, add 1 to the place value you're rounding to and put zero for all digits on its right side. If the digit to the right of the place value is less than 5, keep the place value and put zero for all digits to the right.*

Examples:

1) Round 23 to the nearest ten.

The place value of ten is 2. The digit on the right side is 3 (which is less than 5). Keep 2 and put zero for the digit on the right side. The answer is 20. 23 rounded to the nearest ten is 20, because 23 is closer to 20 than to 30.

2) Round 475 to the nearest hundred.

475 rounded to the nearest hundred is 500, because the digit on the right side of hundred place is 7. Add 1 to 4 and put zeros for other digits. The answer is 500.

✍ *Round each number to the nearest ten.*

1) 23 = ____
2) 16 = ____
3) 35 = ____

4) 48 = ____
5) 71 = ____
6) 99 = ____

✍ *Round each number to the nearest hundred.*

7) 110 = ____
8) 119 = ____
9) 158 = ____

10) 109 = ____
11) 345 = ____
12) 670 = ____

Whole Number Addition and Subtraction

Step-by-step guide:

- ✓ Line up the numbers.
- ✓ Start with the unit place. (ones place)
- ✓ Regroup if necessary.
- ✓ Add or subtract the tens place.
- ✓ Continue with other digits.

Examples:

1) Find the sum. $485 + 245 = ?$

First line up the numbers: $\begin{array}{r} 485 \\ +245 \\ \hline \end{array}$ → Start with the unit place. (ones place) $5 + 5 = 10$,

Write 0 for ones place and keep 1, $\begin{array}{r} 1 \\ 485 \\ +245 \\ \hline 0 \end{array}$, Add the tens place and the digit 1 we kept:

$1 + 8 + 4 = 13$, Write 3 and keep 1, $\begin{array}{r} 1\,1 \\ 485 \\ +245 \\ \hline 30 \end{array}$

Continue with other digits → $1 + 4 + 2 = 7$ → $\begin{array}{r} 1\,1 \\ 485 \\ +245 \\ \hline 730 \end{array}$

2) Find the difference. $576 - 353 = ?$

First line up the numbers: $\begin{array}{r} 576 \\ -353 \\ \hline \end{array}$, → Start with the unit place. $6 - 3 = 3$, $\begin{array}{r} 576 \\ -353 \\ \hline 3 \end{array}$,

Subtract the tens place. $7 - 5 = 2$, $\begin{array}{r} 576 \\ -353 \\ \hline 23 \end{array}$, Continue with other digits → $5 - 3 = 2$, $\begin{array}{r} 576 \\ -453 \\ \hline 223 \end{array}$

✍ *Find the sum or difference.*

1) $1,122 + 577 =$

2) $1,850 - 1,600 =$

3) $1,900 - 1,237 =$

4) $2,550 + 1,800 =$

5) $3,220 + 2,560 =$

6) $2,590 + 2,120 =$

7) $4,823 + 2,891 =$

8) $4,731 + 2,561 =$

Whole Number Multiplication

Step-by-step guide:

✓ Learn the times tables first! To solve multiplication problems fast, you need to memorize the times table. For example, 3 times 8 is 24 or 8 times 7 is 56.

✓ For multiplication, line up the numbers you are multiplying.

✓ Start with the ones place and regroup if necessary.

✓ Continue with other digits.

Examples:

1) Solve. $200 \times 10 = ?$

Line up the numbers: $\begin{array}{r} 200 \\ \times\,10 \\ \hline \end{array}$, start with the ones place → $0 \times 200 = 0$, $\begin{array}{r} 200 \\ \times\,10 \\ \hline 0 \end{array}$, Continue with other digit which is 1. → $200 \times 1 = 200$, $\begin{array}{r} 200 \\ \times\,10 \\ \hline 2{,}000 \end{array}$

2) Solve. $120 \times 15 = ?$

Line up the numbers: $\begin{array}{r} 120 \\ \times\,15 \\ \hline \end{array}$, start with the ones place → $5 \times 0 = 0$, $\begin{array}{r} 120 \\ \times\,15 \\ \hline 0 \end{array}$, $5 \times 2 = 10$, write 0 and keep 1. $\begin{array}{r} 120 \\ \times\,15 \\ \hline 00 \end{array}$, → $5 \times 1 = 5$, add 1 to 5, the answer is 6. $\begin{array}{r} 120 \\ \times\,15 \\ \hline 600 \end{array}$

Now, write 0 in the next line and multiply 120 by 1, using the same process. (Since 1 is in the tens place, we need to write 0 before doing the operation). The answer is 1,200. Add 600 and 1,200. The answer is: $600 + 1{,}200 = 1{,}800$

✍ *Find the missing number.*

1) $15 \times 6 = $ _____

2) $19 \times 7 = $ _____

3) $260 \times 9 = $ _____

4) $300 \times 12 = $ _____

5) $150 \times 50 = $ _____

6) $230 \times 20 = $ _____

7) $432 \times 25 = $ _____

8) $390 \times 34 = $ _____

Whole Number Division

Step-by-step guide:

Division: A typical division problem: Dividend ÷ Divisor = Quotient

- In division, we want to find how many times a number (divisor) is contained in another number (dividend). The result in a division problem is the quotient.

✓ First, write the problem in division format. (dividend is inside; divisor is outside)

$$\text{Divisor} \overline{\smash{)}\text{Dividend}}^{\text{Quotient}}$$

✓ Now, find how many times divisor goes into dividend. (if it is a big number, break the dividend into smaller numbers by choosing the appropriate number of digits from left. Start from the first digit on the left side of the divided and see if the divisor will go into it. If not, keep moving over one digit to the right in the dividend until you have a number the divisor will go into.

✓ Find number of times the divisor goes into the part of the dividend you chose.

✓ Write the answer above the digit in the dividend you are using and multiply it by the divisor and Write the product under the part of the dividend you are using, then subtract.

✓ Bring down the next digit in the dividend and repeat this process until you have nothing left to bring down.

Example: Solve. $234 \div 4 = ?$

$$4 \overline{\smash{)}234}$$

✓ First, write the problem in division format.

✓ Start from left digit of the dividend. 4 doesn't go into 2. So, choose another digit of the dividend. It is 3.

✓ Now, find how many times 4 goes into 23. The answer is 5.

✓ Write 5 above the dividend part. 4 times 5 is 20. Write 20 below 23 and subtract. The answer is 3.

$$4 \overline{\smash{)}234}^{5}$$

✓ Now bring down the next digit which is 4. How many times 4 goes into 34? The answer is 8. Write 8 above dividend. This is the final step since there is no other digit of the dividend to bring down. The final answer is 58 and the remainder is 2.

$$
\begin{array}{r}
58 \\
4 \overline{\smash{)}234} \\
-20 \\
\hline
34 \\
-32 \\
\hline
2
\end{array}
$$

✎ **Solve.**

1) $150 \div 5 = $ _____

2) $360 \div 6 = $ _____

3) $840 \div 7 = $ _____

4) $640 \div 8 = $ _____

5) $240 \div 6 = $ _____

6) $345 \div 8 = $ _____

Rounding and Estimates

Step-by-step guide:

Rounding and estimating are math strategies used for approximating a number. To estimate means to make a rough guess or calculation. To round means to simplify a known number by scaling it slightly up or down.

- ✓ To estimate a math operation, round the numbers.
- ✓ For 2-digit numbers, your usually can round to the nearest tens, for 3-digit numbers, round to nearest hundreds, etc.
- ✓ Find the answer.

Examples:

1) Estimate the sum by rounding each number to the nearest hundred. $145 + 489 =?$
   145 rounded to the nearest hundred is 100. 489 rounded to the nearest hundred is 500.
   Then: $100 + 500 = 600$

2) Estimate the result by rounding each number to the nearest ten. $55 - 43 = ?$
   55 rounded to the nearest ten is 60. 43 rounded to the nearest ten is 40.
   Then: $55 - 40 = 15$

✎ *Estimate the sum by rounding each number to the nearest ten.*

1) $12 + 26 = $ _____

2) $28 + 18 = $ _____

3) $31 + 37 = $ _____

4) $56 + 68 = $ _____

5) $232 + 191 = $ _____

6) $584 + 344 = $ _____

✎ *Estimate the product by rounding each number to the nearest ten.*

7) $13 \times 18 = $ _____

8) $15 \times 25 = $ _____

9) $32 \times 27 = $ _____

10) $48 \times 23 = $ _____

11) $69 \times 35 = $ _____

12) $77 \times 54 = $ _____

Answers – Chapter 1

Rounding

1) 20	5) 70	9) 200
2) 20	6) 100	10) 100
3) 40	7) 100	11) 300
4) 50	8) 100	12) 700

Whole Number Addition and Subtraction

1) 1,699	4) 4,350	7) 7,714
2) 250	5) 5,780	8) 7,292
3) 663	6) 4,710	

Whole Number Multiplication

1) 90	4) 3,600	7) 10,800
2) 133	5) 7,500	8) 13,260
3) 2,340	6) 4,600	

Whole Number Division

1) 30	3) 120	5) 45
2) 60	4) 80	6) $43, r1$

Rounding and Estimates

1) 40	5) 420	9) 900
2) 50	6) 900	10) 1,000
3) 70	7) 200	11) 2,800
4) 130	8) 600	12) 4,000

Chapter 2:
Fractions and Mixed Numbers

Math Topics that you'll learn Chapter:

- ✓ Simplifying Fractions

- ✓ Adding and Subtracting Fractions

- ✓ Multiplying and Dividing Fractions

- ✓ Adding Mixed Numbers

- ✓ Subtracting Mixed Numbers

- ✓ Multiplying Mixed Numbers

- ✓ Dividing Mixed Numbers

"A Man is like a fraction whose numerator is what he is and whose denominator is what he thinks of himself.
The larger the denominator, the smaller the fraction." ~Tolstoy

Simplifying Fractions

Step-by-step guide:

- ✓ Evenly divide both the top and bottom of the fraction by $2, 3, 5, 7, \ldots$ etc.
- ✓ Continue until you can't go any further.

Examples:

1) Simplify $\frac{18}{24}$.

To simplify $\frac{18}{24}$, find a number that both 18 and 24 are divisible by. Both are divisible by 6. Then: $\frac{18}{24} = \frac{18 \div 6}{24 \div 6} = \frac{3}{4}$

2) Simplify $\frac{72}{90}$.

To simplify $\frac{72}{90}$, find a number that both 72 and 90 are divisible by. Both are divisible by 9 and 18. Then: $\frac{72}{90} = \frac{72 \div 9}{90 \div 9} = \frac{8}{10}$, 8 and 10 are divisible by 2, then: $\frac{8}{10} = \frac{4}{5}$

or $\frac{72}{90} = \frac{72 \div 18}{90 \div 18} = \frac{4}{5}$

✍ *Simplify each fraction.*

1) $\frac{8}{6} =$

2) $\frac{4}{16} =$

3) $\frac{13}{26} =$

4) $\frac{21}{28} =$

5) $\frac{30}{45} =$

6) $\frac{8}{48} =$

7) $\frac{15}{45} =$

8) $\frac{22}{26} =$

9) $\frac{28}{54} =$

10) $\frac{35}{75} =$

11) $\frac{49}{63} =$

12) $\frac{38}{50} =$

Adding and Subtracting Fractions

Step-by-step guide:

- ✓ For "like" fractions (fractions with the same denominator), add or subtract the numerators and write the answer over the common denominator.
- ✓ Find equivalent fractions with the same denominator before you can add or subtract fractions with different denominators.
- ✓ Adding and Subtracting with the same denominator:

$$\frac{a}{b} + \frac{c}{b} = \frac{a+c}{b} \ , \frac{a}{b} - \frac{c}{b} = \frac{a-c}{b}$$

- ✓ Adding and Subtracting fractions with different denominators:

$$\frac{a}{b} + \frac{c}{d} = \frac{ad + bc}{bd} \ , \frac{a}{b} - \frac{c}{d} = \frac{ad - cb}{bd}$$

Examples:

1) Subtract fractions. $\frac{2}{3} - \frac{1}{2} =$

For "like" fractions, subtract the numerators and write the answer over the common denominator. then: $\frac{4}{6} - \frac{3}{6} = \frac{4-3}{6} = \frac{1}{6}$

2) Subtract fractions. $\frac{3}{7} + \frac{2}{3} =$

For "unlike" fractions, find equivalent fractions with the same denominator before you can add or subtract fractions with different denominators. Use this formula: $\frac{a}{b} - \frac{c}{d} = \frac{ad - cb}{bd}$

$\frac{3}{7} + \frac{2}{3} = \frac{(3)(3)+(2)(7)}{7 \times 3} = \frac{9+14}{21} = \frac{23}{21}$

✎ *Find the sum or difference.*

1) $\frac{4}{5} + \frac{2}{3} =$

2) $\frac{1}{4} + \frac{1}{3} =$

3) $\frac{3}{2} - \frac{1}{8} =$

4) $\frac{2}{5} - \frac{1}{3} =$

5) $\frac{3}{4} + \frac{5}{4} =$

6) $\frac{4}{7} + \frac{2}{3} =$

7) $\frac{4}{7} - \frac{1}{3} =$

8) $\frac{6}{7} - \frac{3}{5} =$

9) $\frac{3}{8} + \frac{1}{7} =$

Multiplying and Dividing Fractions

Step-by-step guide:

- ✓ Multiplying fractions: multiply the top numbers and multiply the bottom numbers.
- ✓ Dividing fractions: Keep, Change, Flip
- ✓ Keep first fraction, change division sign to multiplication, and flip the numerator and denominator of the second fraction. Then, solve!

Examples:

1) Multiplying fractions. $\frac{2}{5} \times \frac{3}{4} =$

Multiply the top numbers and multiply the bottom numbers.

$\frac{2}{5} \times \frac{3}{4} = \frac{2 \times 3}{5 \times 4} = \frac{6}{20}$, simplify: $\frac{6}{20} = \frac{6 \div 2}{20 \div 2} = \frac{3}{10}$

2) Dividing fractions. $\frac{1}{2} \div \frac{3}{5} =$

Keep first fraction, change division sign to multiplication, and flip the numerator and denominator of the second fraction. Then: $\frac{1}{2} \times \frac{5}{3} = \frac{1 \times 5}{2 \times 3} = \frac{5}{6}$

✎ *Find the answers.*

1) $\frac{1}{3} \times \frac{5}{4} =$

2) $\frac{1}{7} \times \frac{3}{4} =$

3) $\frac{1}{5} \div \frac{1}{4} =$

4) $\frac{3}{4} \div \frac{2}{3} =$

5) $\frac{5}{6} \times \frac{1}{4} =$

6) $\frac{3}{8} \times \frac{5}{9} =$

7) $\frac{3}{8} \div \frac{1}{5} =$

8) $\frac{6}{15} \div \frac{1}{2} =$

9) $\frac{2}{7} \div \frac{6}{5} =$

10) $\frac{4}{7} \times \frac{8}{9} =$

11) $\frac{1}{16} \times \frac{4}{5} =$

12) $\frac{8}{15} \div \frac{6}{5} =$

Adding Mixed Numbers

Step-by-step guide:

Use the following steps for both adding and subtracting mixed numbers.

- ✓ Add whole numbers of the mixed numbers.
- ✓ Add the fractions of each mixed number.
- ✓ Find the Least Common Denominator (LCD) if necessary.
- ✓ Add whole numbers and fractions.
- ✓ Write your answer in lowest terms.

Examples:

1) Add mixed numbers. $1\frac{1}{2} + 2\frac{2}{3} =$

Rewriting our equation with parts separated, $1 + \frac{1}{2} + 2 + \frac{2}{3}$, Solving the whole number parts $1 + 2 = 3$, Solving the fraction parts $\frac{1}{2} + \frac{2}{3}$, and rewrite to solve with the equivalent fractions.

$\frac{3}{6} + \frac{4}{6} = \frac{7}{6} = 1\frac{1}{6}$, then Combining the whole and fraction parts $3 + 1 + \frac{1}{6} = 4\frac{1}{6}$

2) Add mixed numbers. $2\frac{1}{4} + 1\frac{2}{5} =$

Rewriting our equation with parts separated, $2 + \frac{1}{4} + 1 + \frac{2}{5}$, Solving the whole number parts $2 + 1 = 3$, Solving the fraction parts $\frac{1}{4} + \frac{2}{5}$, and rewrite to solve with the equivalent fractions.

$\frac{5}{20} + \frac{8}{20} = \frac{13}{20}$, then Combining the whole and fraction parts $3 + \frac{13}{20} = 3\frac{13}{20}$

✎ *Find the sum.*

1) $1\frac{1}{2} + 2\frac{2}{3} =$

2) $2\frac{1}{3} + 1\frac{1}{2} =$

3) $1\frac{3}{5} + 2\frac{1}{4} =$

4) $3\frac{2}{5} + 2\frac{1}{3} =$

5) $1\frac{2}{7} + 1\frac{3}{4} =$

6) $3\frac{4}{5} + 2\frac{2}{7} =$

7) $2\frac{1}{2} + 7\frac{3}{8} =$

8) $2\frac{7}{8} + 1\frac{1}{3} =$

9) $2\frac{4}{9} + 6\frac{5}{12} =$

Subtract Mixed Numbers

Step-by-step guide:

Use the following steps for both adding and subtracting mixed numbers.

✓ Subtract the whole number of second mixed number from whole number of the first mixed number.
✓ Subtract the second fraction from the first one.
✓ Find the Least Common Denominator (LCD) if necessary.
✓ Add the result of whole numbers and fractions.
✓ Write your answer in lowest terms.

Examples:

1) Subtract. $2\frac{3}{5} - 1\frac{1}{3} =$

Rewriting our equation with parts separated, $2 + \frac{3}{5} - 1 - \frac{1}{3}$

Solving the whole number parts $2 - 1 = 1$, Solving the fraction parts, $\frac{3}{5} - \frac{1}{3} = \frac{9-5}{15} = \frac{4}{15}$

Combining the whole and fraction parts, $1 + \frac{4}{15} = 1\frac{4}{15}$

2) Subtract. $5\frac{5}{8} - 2\frac{1}{4} =$

Rewriting our equation with parts separated, $5 + \frac{5}{8} - 2 - \frac{1}{4}$

Solving the whole number parts $5 - 2 = 3$, Solving the fraction parts, $\frac{5}{8} - \frac{1}{4} = \frac{20-8}{32} = \frac{12}{32}$

Combining the whole and fraction parts, $3 + \frac{12}{32} = 3\frac{12}{32}$

✍ *Find the difference.*

1) $1\frac{2}{3} - 1\frac{1}{2} =$

2) $2\frac{1}{4} - 1\frac{1}{5} =$

3) $3\frac{3}{4} - 2\frac{2}{3} =$

4) $4\frac{5}{6} - 2\frac{2}{3} =$

5) $5\frac{3}{5} - 2\frac{1}{4} =$

6) $6\frac{3}{7} - 1\frac{2}{5} =$

7) $4\frac{4}{9} - 2\frac{2}{3} =$

8) $9\frac{3}{10} - 4\frac{1}{3} =$

9) $12\frac{3}{8} - 8\frac{5}{12} =$

Multiplying Mixed Numbers

Step-by-step guide:

- ✓ Convert the mixed numbers to improper fractions. (improper fraction is a fraction in which the top number is bigger than bottom number)
- ✓ Multiply fractions and simplify if necessary.

$$a\frac{c}{b} = a + \frac{c}{b} = \frac{ab + c}{b}$$

Examples:

1) Multiply mixed numbers. $2\frac{1}{4} \times 3\frac{1}{2} =$

Converting mixed numbers to fractions, $2\frac{1}{4} = \frac{9}{4}$ and $3\frac{1}{2} = \frac{7}{2}$.

$\frac{9}{4} \times \frac{7}{2}$, Applying the fractions formula for multiplication, $\frac{9\times7}{4\times2} = \frac{63}{8} = 7\frac{7}{8}$

2) Multiply mixed numbers. $5\frac{2}{3} \times 3\frac{3}{4} =$

Converting mixed numbers to fractions, $\frac{17}{3} \times \frac{15}{4}$, Applying the fractions formula for multiplication, $\frac{17\times15}{3\times4} = \frac{85}{4} = 21\frac{1}{4}$

✎ *Find the product.*

1) $1\frac{1}{2} \times 2\frac{1}{4} =$

2) $1\frac{2}{3} \times 1\frac{3}{4} =$

3) $4\frac{2}{5} \times 2\frac{1}{2} =$

4) $3\frac{1}{6} \times 1\frac{2}{3} =$

5) $3\frac{2}{7} \times 2\frac{1}{5} =$

6) $4\frac{2}{3} \times 3\frac{1}{7} =$

7) $5\frac{3}{8} \times 2\frac{3}{4} =$

8) $3\frac{4}{7} \times 7\frac{2}{9} =$

9) $8\frac{3}{5} \times 4\frac{3}{8} =$

10) $6\frac{5}{7} \times 2\frac{5}{9} =$

Dividing Mixed Numbers

Step-by-step guide:

✓ Convert the mixed numbers to improper fractions.

✓ Divide fractions and simplify if necessary.

$$a\frac{c}{b} = a + \frac{c}{b} = \frac{ab+c}{b}$$

Examples:

1) Find the quotient. $2\frac{1}{3} \div 1\frac{1}{4} =$

Converting mixed numbers to fractions, $\frac{7}{3} \div \frac{5}{4}$, Applying the fractions formula for multiplication, $\frac{7\times4}{3\times5} = \frac{28}{15} = 1\frac{13}{15}$

2) Find the quotient. $2\frac{5}{6} \div 1\frac{2}{5} =$

Converting mixed numbers to fractions, $\frac{17}{6} \div \frac{7}{5}$, Applying the fractions formula for multiplication, $\frac{17\times5}{6\times7} = \frac{85}{42} = 2\frac{1}{42}$

✍ *Find the quotient.*

1) $3\frac{1}{3} \div 2\frac{1}{2} =$

2) $2\frac{1}{2} \div 1\frac{1}{4} =$

3) $4\frac{3}{4} \div 2\frac{2}{3} =$

4) $3\frac{1}{6} \div 2\frac{2}{3} =$

5) $5\frac{1}{4} \div 2\frac{3}{5} =$

6) $2\frac{2}{7} \div 2\frac{1}{4} =$

7) $1\frac{4}{9} \div 2\frac{1}{3} =$

8) $7\frac{4}{5} \div 3\frac{2}{3} =$

9) $6\frac{3}{4} \div 2\frac{2}{5} =$

10) $8\frac{4}{7} \div 3\frac{5}{6} =$

Answers – Day 2

Simplifying Fractions

1) $\frac{4}{3}$

2) $\frac{1}{4}$

3) $\frac{1}{2}$

4) $\frac{3}{4}$

5) $\frac{2}{3}$

6) $\frac{1}{6}$

7) $\frac{1}{3}$

8) $\frac{11}{13}$

9) $\frac{14}{27}$

10) $\frac{7}{15}$

11) $\frac{7}{9}$

12) $\frac{19}{25}$

Adding and Subtracting Fractions

1) $\frac{22}{15}$

2) $\frac{7}{12}$

3) $\frac{11}{8}$

4) $\frac{1}{15}$

5) 2

6) $\frac{26}{21}$

7) $\frac{5}{21}$

8) $\frac{9}{35}$

9) $\frac{29}{56}$

Multiplying and Dividing Fractions

1) $\frac{5}{12}$

2) $\frac{3}{28}$

3) $\frac{4}{5}$

4) $\frac{9}{8}$

5) $\frac{5}{24}$

6) $\frac{5}{24}$

7) $\frac{15}{8}$

8) $\frac{4}{5}$

9) $\frac{5}{21}$

10) $\frac{32}{63}$

11) $\frac{1}{20}$

12) $\frac{4}{9}$

Adding Mixed Numbers

1) $4\frac{1}{6}$

2) $3\frac{5}{6}$

3) $3\frac{17}{20}$

4) $5\frac{11}{15}$

5) $3\frac{1}{28}$

6) $6\frac{3}{35}$

7) $9\frac{7}{8}$

8) $4\frac{5}{24}$

9) $8\frac{31}{36}$

Subtract Mixed Numbers

1) $\frac{1}{6}$

2) $1\frac{1}{20}$

3) $1\frac{1}{12}$

4) $2\frac{1}{6}$

5) $3\frac{7}{20}$

6) $5\frac{1}{35}$

7) $1\frac{7}{9}$

8) $4\frac{29}{30}$

9) $3\frac{23}{24}$

Multiplying Mixed Numbers

1) $3\frac{3}{8}$

2) $2\frac{11}{12}$

3) 11

4) $5\frac{5}{18}$

5) $7\frac{8}{35}$

6) $14\frac{2}{3}$

7) $14\frac{25}{32}$

8) $25\frac{50}{63}$

9) $37\frac{5}{8}$

10) $17\frac{10}{63}$

Dividing Mixed Numbers

1) $1\frac{1}{3}$

2) 2

3) $1\frac{25}{32}$

4) $1\frac{3}{16}$

5) $2\frac{1}{52}$

6) $1\frac{1}{63}$

7) $\frac{13}{21}$

8) $2\frac{7}{55}$

9) $2\frac{13}{16}$

10) $2\frac{38}{161}$

Chapter 3:
Decimals

Math Topics that you'll learn Chapter:

- ✓ Comparing Decimals

- ✓ Rounding Decimals

- ✓ Adding and Subtracting Decimals

- ✓ Multiplying and Dividing Decimals

"Do not worry about your difficulties in mathematics. I can assure you mine are still greater." ~ Albert Einstein

Comparing Decimals

Step-by-step guide:

Decimals: is a fraction written in a special form. For example, instead of writing $\frac{1}{2}$ you can write **0.5**.

For comparing decimals:

✓ Compare each digit of two decimals in the same place value.
✓ Start from left. Compare hundreds, tens, ones, tenth, hundredth, etc.
✓ To compare numbers, use these symbols:
- Equal to =,   Less than <,   Greater than >
    Greater than or equal ≥,   Less than or equal ≤

Examples:

1) Compare 0.40 and 0.04.

   0.40 *is greater than* 0.04, because the tenth place of 0.40 is 4, but the tenth place of 0.04 is zero. Then: $0.40 > 0.04$

2) Compare 0.0912 and 0.912.

   0.912 *is greater than* 0.0912, because the tenth place of 0.912 is 9, but the tenth place of 0.0912 is zero. Then: $0.0912 < 0.912$

✍ *Write the correct comparison symbol (>, < or =).*

1) 0.70 ☐ 0.070

2) 0.018 ☐ 0.18

3) 1.050 ☐ 1.05

4) 2.75 ☐ 2.07

5) 1.05 ☐ 0.550

6) 4.05 ☐ 4.5

7) 7.05 ☐ 7.050

8) 12.02 ☐ 12.1

9) 8.45 ☐ 8.125

10) 0.813 ☐ 0.0813

11) 14.15 ☐ 14.150

12) 0.678 ☐ 0.687

Rounding Decimals

Step-by-step guide:

- ✓ We can round decimals to a certain accuracy or number of decimal places. This is used to make calculation easier to do and results easier to understand, when exact values are not too important.
- ✓ First, you'll need to remember your place values: For example:

$$12.4567$$

1: tens	2: ones	4: tenths
5: hundredths	6: thousandths	7: tens thousandths

- ✓ To round a decimal, find the place value you'll round to.
- ✓ Find the digit to the right of the place value you're rounding to. If it is 5 or bigger, add 1 to the place value you're rounding to and remove all digits on its right side. If the digit to the right of the place value is less than 5, keep the place value and remove all digits on the right.

Examples:

1) Round **1.9278** to the thousandth place value.

First look at the next place value to the right, (tens thousandths). It's 8 and it is greater than 5. Thus add 1 to the digit in the thousandth place.

Thousandth place is 7. → 7 + 1 = 8, then, the answer is 1.928

2) **9.4126** rounded to the nearest hundredth.

First look at the next place value to the right of thousandths. It's 2 and it is less than 5, thus remove all the digits to the right. Then, the answer is 9.41.

✍ *Round each decimal to the nearest whole number.*

1) 12.22	3) 11.45	5) 9.95
2) 9.5	4) 24.5	6) 77.8

✍ *Round each decimal to the nearest tenth.*

7) 14.352	9) 34.428	11) 1.7925
8) 10.569	10) 67.249	12) 23.319

Adding and Subtracting Decimals

Step-by-step guide:

✓ Line up the numbers.

✓ Add zeros to have same number of digits for both numbers if necessary.

✓ Add or subtract using column addition or subtraction.

Examples:

1) Add. $1.5 + 2.14 =$

First line up the numbers: $\begin{array}{r} 1.5 \\ + 2.14 \\ \hline \end{array}$ → Add zeros to have same number of digits for both

numbers. $\begin{array}{r} 1.50 \\ + 2.14 \\ \hline \end{array}$, Start with the hundredths place. $0 + 4 = 4$, $\begin{array}{r} 1.50 \\ + 2.14 \\ \hline 4 \end{array}$, Continue with tenths

place. $5 + 1 = 6$, $\begin{array}{r} 1.50 \\ + 2.14 \\ \hline .64 \end{array}$. Add the ones place. $2 + 1 = 3$, $\begin{array}{r} 1.50 \\ + 2.14 \\ \hline 3.64 \end{array}$

2) Subtract decimals. $2.56 - 1.15 =$ $\begin{array}{r} 2.56 \\ - 1.15 \\ \hline \end{array}$

Start with the hundredths place. $6 - 5 = 1$, $\begin{array}{r} 2.56 \\ - 1.15 \\ \hline 1 \end{array}$, continue with tenths place. $5 - 1 = 4$

$\begin{array}{r} 2.56 \\ - 1.15 \\ \hline .41 \end{array}$, subtract the ones place. $2 - 1 = 1$, $\begin{array}{r} 2.56 \\ - 1.15 \\ \hline 1.41 \end{array}$.

✎ *Find the sum or difference.*

1) $18.24 - 12.20 =$

2) $21.50 + 17.77 =$

3) $13.98 + 11.78 =$

4) $66.34 - 48.50 =$

5) $53.12 + 15.25 =$

6) $78.90 - 23.61 =$

7) $82.24 - 65.55 =$

8) $93.75 + 82.63 =$

Multiplying and Dividing Decimals

Step-by-step guide:

For Multiplication:

✓ Ignore the decimal point and set up and multiply the numbers as you do with whole numbers.
Count the total number of decimal places in both of the factors.
Place the decimal point in the product.
For Division:

✓ If the divisor is not a whole number, move decimal point to right to make it a whole number. Do the same for dividend.
✓ Divide similar to whole numbers.

Examples:

1) Find the product. $0.60 \times 0.20 =$

Set up and multiply the numbers as you do with whole numbers. Line up the numbers: $\begin{smallmatrix} 60 \\ \times 20 \end{smallmatrix}$, Start with

the ones place → $60 \times 0 = 0$, $\begin{smallmatrix} 60 \\ \times 20 \\ \hline 0 \end{smallmatrix}$, Continue with other digits → $60 \times 2 = 120$, $\begin{smallmatrix} 60 \\ \times 20 \\ \hline 1,200 \end{smallmatrix}$, Count the

total number of decimal places in both of the factors. (4). Then Place the decimal point in the product.

Then: $\begin{smallmatrix} 0.60 \\ \times 0.20 \\ \hline 0.1200 \end{smallmatrix}$ → $0.60 \times 0.20 = 0.12$

2) Find the quotient. $1.40 \div 0.2 =$
The divisor is not a whole number. Multiply it by 10 to get 2. Do the same for the dividend to get 14.
Now, divide: $14 \div 2 = 7$. The answer is 7.

✍ *Find the product and quotient.*

1) $0.2 \times 0.5 =$

2) $1.5 \times 0.8 =$

3) $0.25 \times 0.5 =$

4) $0.15 \times 0.30 =$

5) $1.12 \times 0.4 =$

6) $0.34 \times 0.5 =$

7) $2.25 \div 0.5 =$

8) $62.2 \div 1,000 =$

9) $8.42 \div 2 =$

10) $8.6 \div 0.4 =$

11) $42.6 \div 0.2 =$

12) $86.5 \div 5 =$

Answers – Chapter 3

Comparing Decimals

1) >	7) =
2) <	8) <
3) =	9) >
4) >	10) >
5) >	11) =
6) <	12) <

Rounding Decimals

1) 12	5) 10	9) 34.4
2) 10	6) 78	10) 67.2
3) 11	7) 14.4	11) 1.8
4) 25	8) 10.6	12) 23.3

Adding and Subtracting Decimals

1) 6.04	4) 17.84	7) 16.69
2) 39.27	5) 68.37	8) 176.38
3) 25.76	6) 55.29	

Multiplying and Dividing Decimals

1) 0.1	5) 0.448	9) 4.21
2) 1.2	6) 0.17	10) 21.5
3) 0.125	7) 4.5	11) 213
4) 0.045	8) 0.0622	12) 17.3

Chapter 4:
Factoring Numbers

Math Topics that you'll learn Chapter:

- ✓ Factoring Numbers

- ✓ Greatest Common Factor

- ✓ Least Common Multiple

"The study of mathematics, like the Nile, begins in minuteness but ends in magnificence."

- Charles Caleb Colton

Factoring Numbers

Step-by-step guide:

- ✓ Factoring numbers means to break the numbers into their prime factors.
- ✓ First few prime numbers: $2, 3, 5, 7, 11, 13, 17, 19$

Examples:

1) List all positive factors of 8.

   Write the upside-down division:
   The second column is the answer.
   Then: $8 = 2 \times 2 \times 2$ or $8 = 2^3$

8	2
4	2
2	2
1	

2) List all positive factors of 24.

   Write the upside-down division:
   The second column is the answer.
   Then: $24 = 2 \times 2 \times 2 \times 3$
   or $20 = 2^3 \times 3$

24	2
12	2
6	2
3	3
1	

✍ *List all positive factors of each number.*

1) 4	5) 16	9) 36
2) 6	6) 18	10) 38
3) 9	7) 24	11) 42
4) 12	8) 28	12) 56

Greatest Common Factor

Step-by-step guide:

- ✓ List the prime factors of each number.
- ✓ Multiply common prime factors.
- ✓ If there are no common prime factors, the GCF is 1.

Examples:

1) Find the GCF for 8 and 12.

   The factors of 8 are: $\{1, 2, 4, 8\}$

   The factors of 12 are: $\{1, 2, 3, 4, 6, 12\}$

   There is 4 in common,

   Then the greatest common factor is: 4.

2) Find the GCF for 14 and 18.

   The factors of 8 are: $\{1, 2, 7, 14\}$

   The factors of 20 are: $\{1, 2, 3, 6, 9, 18\}$

   There is 2 in common.

   Then the greatest common factor is: 2.

✎ *Find the GCF for each number pair.*

1) 6, 2	5) 4, 10	9) 15, 12
2) 4, 8	6) 6, 18	10) 14, 20
3) 5, 10	7) 9, 24	11) 12, 26
4) 8, 12	8) 16, 14	12) 22, 32

Least Common Multiple

Step-by-step guide:

- ✓ Least Common Multiple is the smallest multiple that 2 or more numbers have in common.
- ✓ How to find LCM: list out all the multiples of each number and then find the first one they have in common,

Examples:

1) Find the LCM for 8 and 6.

Multiples of 8: 8, 16, 24, ...

Multiples of 6: 6, 12, 18, 24, ...

$LCM = 24$

2) Find the LCM for 4 and 12.

Multiples of 4: 4, 8, 12, 16, 20, ...

Multiples of 12: 12, 24, 36, 48

$LCM = 12$

✎ *Find the LCM for each number pair.*

1) 2, 4	5) 8, 16	9) 6, 22
2) 3, 6	6) 12, 8	10) 14, 28
3) 6, 8	7) 4, 12	11) 16, 18
4) 7, 12	8) 5, 20	12) 24, 32

Answers – Chapter 4

Factoring Numbers

1) 2×2
2) 2×3
3) 3×3
4) $2 \times 2 \times 3$
5) $2 \times 2 \times 2 \times 2$
6) $2 \times 3 \times 3$

7) $2 \times 2 \times 2 \times 3$
8) $2 \times 2 \times 7$
9) $2 \times 2 \times 3 \times 3$
10) 2×19
11) $2 \times 3 \times 7$
12) $2 \times 2 \times 2 \times 7$

Greatest Common Factor

1) 2
2) 4
3) 5
4) 4
5) 2
6) 6

7) 3
8) 2
9) 3
10) 2
11) 2
12) 2

Least Common Multiple

1) 4
2) 6
3) 24
4) 84
5) 16
6) 24

7) 12
8) 20
9) 66
10) 28
11) 144
12) 96

Chapter 5:
Integers and Order of Operations

Math Topics that you'll learn Chapter:

✓ Adding and Subtracting Integers

✓ Multiplying and Dividing Integers

✓ Ordering Integers and Numbers

✓ Order of Operations

✓ Integers and Absolute Value

Without mathematics, there's nothing you can do. Everything around you is mathematics. Everything around you is numbers." - Shakuntala Devi

Adding and Subtracting Integers

Step-by-step guide:

- ✓ Integers includes: zero, counting numbers, and the negative of the counting numbers. $\{\ldots, -3, -2, -1, 0, 1, 2, 3, \ldots\}$
- ✓ Add a positive integer by moving to the right on the number line.
- ✓ Add a negative integer by moving to the left on the number line.
- ✓ Subtract an integer by adding its opposite.

Examples:

1) Solve. $(-2) - (-6) =$

Keep the first number, and convert the sign of the second number to it's opposite. (change subtraction into addition. Then: $(-2) + 6 = 4$

2) Solve. $8 + (12 - 20) =$

First subtract the numbers in brackets, $12 - 20 = -8$

Then: $8 + (-8) = \; \rightarrow$ change addition into subtraction: $8 - 8 = 0$

✍ *Find each sum or difference.*

1) $-(2) + 9 =$

2) $(-4) + (-8) =$

3) $12 + (-18) =$

4) $13 + (-22) =$

5) $2 + (-9) + 3 =$

6) $(-18) + (-4) + 2 =$

7) $4 + (-2) - (-8) =$

8) $5 - (-20 - 12) =$

9) $(-4 + 2) - 6 =$

10) $10 - (-6 + 5) =$

11) $15 - (5 - 3) =$

12) $-(22) - (-13) + 4 =$

Multiplying and Dividing Integers

Step-by-step guide:

Use these rules for multiplying and dividing integers:
- ✓ (negative) × (negative) = positive
- ✓ (negative) ÷ (negative) = positive
- ✓ (negative) × (positive) = negative
- ✓ (negative) ÷ (positive) = negative
- ✓ (positive) × (positive) = positive

Examples:

1) Solve. $3 \times (12 - 14) =$

First subtract the numbers in brackets, $12 - 14 = -2 \rightarrow (3) \times (-2) =$

Now use this formula: (negative) × (positive) = negative
$(3) \times (-2) = -6$

2) Solve. $(-8) + (12 \div 4) =$

First divided 48 by 6 , the numbers in brackets, $12 \div 4 = 3$

$= (-8) + (3) = -8 + 3 = -5$

✎ *Find each product or quotient.*

1) $(-2) \times (9) =$

2) $(-12) \times 3 =$

3) $(-5) \times (-8) =$

4) $(-3) \times (-10) =$

5) $(-4) \times (-3) \times 2 =$

6) $(18 - 3) \times (-5) =$

7) $(16 - 4) \div (-4) =$

8) $(-15) \div (-3) =$

9) $(-48) \div (-6) =$

10) $56 \div (-8) =$

11) $(-121) \div 11 =$

12) $(-128) \div (-4) =$

Ordering Integers and Numbers

Step-by-step guide:

- ✓ When using a number line, numbers increase as you move to the right.
- ✓ When comparing two numbers, think about their position on number line. If one number is on the right side of another number, it is a bigger number. For example, -3 is bigger than -5 because it is on the right side of -5 on number line.

Examples:

1) Order this set of integers from least to greatest. $-4, -1, -5, 4, 2, 7$
The smallest number is -5 and the largest number is 7.

Now compare the integers and order them from least to greatest:
$-5 < -4 < -1 < 2 < 4 < 7$

2) Order each set of integers from greatest to least. $3, -2, -1, 6, -9, 8$
The largest number is 8 and the smallest number is -9.

Now compare the integers and order them from greatest to least:
$8 > 6 > 3 > -1 > -2 > -9$

✎ *Order each set of integers from least to greatest.*

1) $6, -8, -5, 0, 2$ ___, ___, ___, ___, ___, ___
2) $-3, -10, 4, 11, 8$ ___, ___, ___, ___, ___, ___
3) $17, -11, -18, 20, -19$ ___, ___, ___, ___, ___, ___
4) $-14, -24, 17, -6, 31$ ___, ___, ___, ___, ___, ___

✎ *Order each set of integers from greatest to least.*

5) $10, 15, -8, -11, -5$ ___, ___, ___, ___, ___, ___
6) $22, 30, -13, -19, 38$ ___, ___, ___, ___, ___, ___
7) $44, -20, -17, 54, -4$ ___, ___, ___, ___, ___, ___
8) $67, 80, -13, -9, 93$ ___, ___, ___, ___, ___, ___

Order of Operations

Step-by-step guide:

When there is more than one math operation, use PEMDAS:

- ✓ Parentheses
- ✓ Exponents
- ✓ Multiplication and Division (from left to right)
- ✓ Addition and Subtraction (from left to right)

Examples:

1) Solve. $(2 + 4) \div (2^2 \div 4) =$

First simplify inside parentheses: $(6) \div (4 \div 4) = (6) \div (1) =$
Then: $(6) \div (1) = 6$

2) Solve. $(9 \times 6) - (10 - 6) =$

First simplify inside parentheses: $(9 \times 6) - (10 - 6) = (54) - (4) =$

Then: $(54) - (4) = 50$

✍ *Evaluate each expression.*

1) $12 + (3 \times 2) =$

2) $8 - (4 \times 5) =$

3) $(8 \times 2) + 14 =$

4) $(10 - 6) - (4 \times 3) =$

5) $15 + (12 \div 2) =$

6) $(24 \times 3) \div 4 =$

7) $(28 \div 2) \times (-4) =$

8) $(2 \times 6) + (14 - 8) =$

9) $45 + (4 \times 2) + 12 =$

10) $(10 \times 5) \div (4 + 1) =$

11) $(-6) + (8 \times 6) + 10 =$

12) $(12 \times 4) - (56 \div 4) =$

Integers and Absolute Value

Step-by-step guide:

✓ To find an absolute value of a number, just find its distance from 0 on number line! For example, the distance of 12 and -12 from zero on number line is 12!

Examples:

1) Solve. $|8 - 2| \times \frac{|-4 \times 6|}{3} =$

First solve $|8 - 2|$, $\rightarrow |8 - 2| = |6|$, the absolute value of 6 is 6, $|6| = 6$

$6 \times \frac{|-4 \times 6|}{3} =$

Now solve $|-4 \times 6|$, $\rightarrow |-4 \times 6| = |-24|$, the absolute value of -24 is 24, $|-24| = 24$

Then: $6 \times \frac{24}{3} = 6 \times 8 = 48$

2) Solve. $\frac{|-12|}{3} \times |9 - 4| =$

First find $|-12|$, $\rightarrow$ the absolute value of -12 is 12, then: $|-12| = 12$

$\frac{12}{3} \times |9 - 4| =$

Next, solve $|9 - 4|$, $\rightarrow |9 - 4| = |-5|$, the absolute value of -5 is 5. $|-5| = 5$

Then: $\frac{12}{3} \times 5 = 4 \times 5 = 20$

✎ *Evaluate the value.*

1) $2 - |4 - 10| - |8| =$

2) $|7| - \frac{|-14|}{2} =$

3) $\frac{|-18|}{3} \times |-4| =$

4) $\frac{|6 \times -4|}{2} \times \frac{|-28|}{4} =$

5) $|12 \times -2| + \frac{|-56|}{7} =$

6) $\frac{|-40|}{4} \times \frac{|-66|}{11} =$

7) $|-25 + 3| \times \frac{|-8 \times 5|}{2} =$

8) $\frac{|20 \times -3|}{2} \times |-14| =$

Answers – Chapter 5

Adding and Subtracting Integers

1) 7
2) −12
3) −6
4) −9

5) −4
6) −20
7) 10
8) 37

9) −8
10) 11
11) 13
12) −5

Multiplying and Dividing Integers

1) −18
2) −36
3) 40
4) 30

5) 24
6) −75
7) −3
8) 5

9) 8
10) −7
11) −11
12) 32

Ordering Integers and Numbers

1) −8, −5, 0, 2, 6
2) −10, −3, 4, 8, 11
3) −19, −18, −11, 17, 20
4) −24, −14, −6, 17, 31

5) 15, 10, −5, −8, −11
6) 38, 30, 22, −13, −19
7) 54, 44, −4, −17, −20
8) 93, 80, 67, −9, −13

Order of Operations

1) 18
2) −12
3) 30
4) −8

5) 21
6) 18
7) −56
8) 18

9) 65
10) 10
11) 52
12) 34

Integers and Absolute Value

1) −12
2) 0
3) 24

4) 84
5) 32
6) 60

7) 440
8) 420

Chapter 6:

Ratios

Math Topics that you'll learn Chapter:

- ✓ Simplifying Ratios

- ✓ Proportional Ratios

- ✓ Create a Proportion

- ✓ Similarity and Ratios

- ✓ Simple Interest

Mathematics is the door and key to the sciences. ~ Roger Bacon

Simplifying Ratios

Step-by-step guide:

- ✓ Ratios are used to make comparisons between two numbers.
- ✓ Ratios can be written as a fraction, using the word "to", or with a colon.
- ✓ You can calculate equivalent ratios by multiplying or dividing both sides of the ratio by the same number.

Examples:

1) Simplify. $4:2 =$

Both numbers 4 and 2 are divisible by 2 , $\Rightarrow 4 \div 2 = 2, 2 \div 2 = 1,$

Then: $4:2 = 2:1$

2) Simplify. $\frac{14}{24} =$

Both numbers 14 and 24 are divisible by 2, $\Rightarrow 14 \div 2 = 7, 24 \div 2 = 12,$

Then: $\frac{14}{24} = \frac{7}{12}$

✎ *Reduce each ratio.*

1) $4:8 =$ ___ : ___

2) $5:10 =$ ___ : ___

3) $3:9 =$ ___ : ___

4) $8:6 =$ ___ : ___

5) $6:14 =$ ___ : ___

6) $5:25 =$ ___ : ___

7) $16:18 =$ ___ : ___

8) $30:40 =$ ___ : ___

9) $15:50 =$ ___ : ___

10) $14:18 =$ ___ : ___

11) $15:27 =$ ___ : ___

12) $48:24 =$ ___ : ___

Proportional Ratios

Step-by-step guide:

✓ A proportion means that two ratios are equal. It can be written in two ways:
$$\frac{a}{b} = \frac{c}{d}, a : b = c : d$$

✓ The proportion $\frac{a}{b} = \frac{c}{d}$ can be written as: $a \times d = c \times b$

Examples:

1) Solve this proportion for x. $\frac{2}{4} = \frac{3}{x}$

Use cross multiplication: $\frac{2}{4} = \frac{3}{x} \Rightarrow 2 \times x = 3 \times 4 \Rightarrow 2x = 12$

Divide to find x: $x = \frac{12}{2} \Rightarrow x = 6$

2) If a box contains red and blue balls in ratio of $2:5$ red to blue, how many red balls are there if 60 blue balls are in the box?

Write a proportion and solve. $\frac{2}{5} = \frac{x}{60}$

Use cross multiplication: $2 \times 60 = 5 \times x \Rightarrow 120 = 5x$

Divide to find x: $x = \frac{120}{5} \Rightarrow x = 24$

✍ *Solve each proportion.*

1) $\frac{2}{4} = \frac{8}{x}$, $x =$ _____

2) $\frac{1}{2} = \frac{6}{x}$, $x =$ _____

3) $\frac{2}{3} = \frac{12}{x}$, $x =$ _____

4) $\frac{1}{4} = \frac{x}{20}$, $x =$ _____

5) $\frac{3}{4} = \frac{x}{8}$, $x =$ _____

6) $\frac{1}{4} = \frac{18}{x}$, $x =$ _____

7) $\frac{5}{8} = \frac{10}{x}$, $x =$ _____

8) $\frac{6}{9} = \frac{24}{x}$, $x =$ _____

9) $\frac{4}{6} = \frac{x}{18}$, $x =$ _____

10) $\frac{5}{8} = \frac{x}{112}$, $x =$ _____

11) $\frac{3}{18} = \frac{x}{120}$, $x =$ _____

12) $\frac{12}{18} = \frac{x}{96}$, $x =$ _____

Create a Proportion

Step-by-step guide:

✓ A proportion contains two equal fractions! A proportion simply means that two fractions are equal.
✓ To create a proportion, simply find (or create) two equal fractions.

Examples:

1) Express ratios as a Proportion.
180 miles on 9 gallons of gas, how many miles on 1 gallon of gas?

First create a fraction: $\frac{180 \ miles}{9 \ gallons}$, and divide: $180 \div 9 = 20$

Then: 20 miles per gallon

2) State if this pair of ratios form a proportion. $\frac{2}{3} \ and \ \frac{12}{30}$

Use cross multiplication: $\frac{2}{3} = \frac{12}{30} \rightarrow 2 \times 30 = 12 \times 3 \rightarrow 60 = 36$, which is not correct. Therefore, this pair of ratios doesn't form a proportion.

✎ *State if each pair of ratios form a proportion.*

1) $\frac{2}{10} \ and \ \frac{4}{20}$ 5) $\frac{1}{6} \ and \ \frac{8}{48}$ 9) $\frac{6}{17} \ and \ \frac{36}{85}$

2) $\frac{1}{2} \ and \ \frac{15}{25}$ 6) $\frac{5}{6} \ and \ \frac{35}{42}$ 10) $\frac{2}{7} \ and \ \frac{24}{86}$

3) $\frac{4}{9} \ and \ \frac{40}{81}$ 7) $\frac{3}{7} \ and \ \frac{27}{72}$ 11) $\frac{13}{21} \ and \ \frac{182}{294}$

4) $\frac{6}{11} \ and \ \frac{42}{77}$ 8) $\frac{2}{5} \ and \ \frac{16}{45}$ 12) $\frac{12}{19} \ and \ \frac{156}{247}$

Similarity and Ratios

Step-by-step guide:

✓ Two or more figures are similar if the corresponding angles are equal, and the corresponding sides are in proportion.

Examples:

1) A girl 180 *cm* tall, stands 340 *cm* from a lamp post at night. Her shadow from the light is 80 *cm* long. How high is the lamp post?

Write the proportion and solve for missing side.

$$\frac{\text{Smaller triangle height}}{\text{Smaller triangle base}} = \frac{\text{Bigger triangle height}}{\text{Bigger triangle base}}$$

$$\Rightarrow \frac{80cm}{180cm} = \frac{80+340cm}{x} \Rightarrow 80x = 180 \times 420 \Rightarrow x = 945 \ cm$$

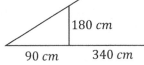

180 *cm*

90 *cm*   340 *cm*

2) A tree 20 *feet* tall casts a shadow 14 *feet* long. Jack is 10 *feet* tall. How long is Jack's shadow?

Write a proportion and solve for the missing number.

$$\frac{20}{14} = \frac{10}{x} \rightarrow 20x = 10 \times 14$$

$$20x = 140 \rightarrow x = \frac{140}{20} = 7$$

✎ *Each pair of figures is similar. Find the missing side.*

1)

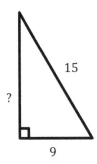

15

?

9

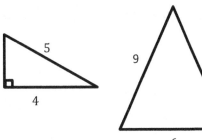

5

3

4

9   9

6

3   3

?

3)

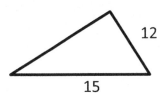

12

15

4

?

4)

?

8

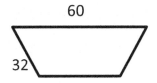

60

32

Simple Interest

Step-by-step guide:

✓ Simple Interest: The charge for borrowing money or the return for lending it. To solve a simple interest problem, use this formula:

Interest = principal × rate × time $\Rightarrow$ $I = p \times r \times t$

Examples:

1) Find simple interest for $450 investment at 7% for 8 years.

Use Interest formula: $I = prt$

$P = \$450$, r $= 7\% = \dfrac{7}{100} = 0.07$ and $t = 8$

Then: $I = 450 \times 0.07 \times 8 = \$252$

2) Find simple interest for $5,200 at 4% for 3 years.

Use Interest formula: $I = prt$

$P = \$5,200$, r $= 4\% = \dfrac{4}{100} = 0.04$ and $t = 3$

Then: $I = 5,200 \times 0.04 \times 3 = \$624$

✎ *Determine the simple interest for these loans.*

1) $840 at 6% for 4 years. $ _____

2) $2,500 at 2% for 8 years. $ _____

3) $1,200 at 4% for 5 years. $ _____

4) $4,000 at 1.5% for 3 years. $ _____

5) $5,300 at 3% for 2 years. $ _____

6) $1,200 at 5.5% for 4 years. $ _____

7) $1,800 at 5% for 6 months. $ _____

8) $20,000 at 2.5% for 7 years. $ _____

Answers – Chapter 6

Simplifying Ratios

1) $1:2$
2) $1:2$
3) $1:3$
4) $4:3$

5) $3:7$
6) $1:5$
7) $8:9$
8) $3:4$

9) $3:10$
10) $7:9$
11) $5:9$
12) $2:1$

Proportional Ratios

1) 16
2) 12
3) 18
4) 5

5) 6
6) 72
7) 16
8) 36

9) 12
10) 70
11) 20
12) 96

Create a Proportion

1) Yes
2) No
3) No
4) Yes

5) Yes
6) Yes
7) Yes
8) *No*

9) No
10) No
11) Yes
12) Yes

Similarity and ratios

1) 12
2) 2

3) 5
4) 15

Simple Interest

1) $201.60
2) $400
3) $240
4) $180

5) $318
6) $264
7) $45
8) $3,500

Chapter 7:
Percentage

Math Topics that you'll learn Chapter:

✓ Percentage Calculations

✓ Percent Problems

✓ Percent of Increase and Decrease

✓ Discount, Tax and Tip

Mathematics is no more computation than typing is literature.

- John Allen Paulos

Percentage Calculations

Step-by-step guide:

- ✓ Percent is a ratio of a number and 100. It always has the same denominator, 100. Percent symbol is %.
- ✓ Percent is another way to write decimals or fractions. For example:

$$40\% = 0.40 = \frac{40}{100} = \frac{2}{5}$$

- ✓ Use the following formula to find part, whole, or percent:

$$\text{part} = \frac{\text{percent}}{100} \times \text{whole}$$

Examples:

1) What is 15% of 50? Use the following formula: $\text{part} = \frac{\text{percent}}{100} \times \text{whole}$

$\text{part} = \frac{15}{100} \times 50 \;\rightarrow\; \text{part} = \frac{15 \times 50}{100} \;\rightarrow\; \text{part} = \frac{75}{10} \;\rightarrow\; \text{part} = 7.5$

2) What is 30% of 35? Use the percent formula: $part = \frac{percent}{100} \times whole$

$\text{part} = \frac{30}{100} \times 35 \;\rightarrow\; \text{part} = \frac{105}{10} \;\rightarrow\; \text{part} = 10.5$

✍ *Calculate the given percent of each value.*

1) 10% of 100 = ____

2) 50% of 40 = ____

3) 20% of 50 = ____

4) 30% of 70 = ____

5) 45% of 20 = ____

6) 50% of 80 = ____

7) 30% of 100 = ____

8) 15% of 60 = ____

9) 40% of 90 = ____

10) 29% of 86 = ____

11) 33% of 54 = ____

12) 71% of 112 = ____

Percent Problems

Step-by-step guide:

- ✓ In each percent problem, we are looking for the base, or part or the percent.
- ✓ Use the following equations to find each missing section.
    - ○ Base = Part ÷ Percent
    - ○ Part = Percent × Base
    - ○ Percent = Part ÷ Base

Examples:

1) 2.5 is what percent of 20?

In this problem, we are looking for the percent. Use the following equation:
$$Percent = Part \div Base \rightarrow Percent = 2.5 \div 20 = 0.125 = 12.5\%$$

2) 40 is 10% of what number?

Use the following formula: $Base = Part \div Percent \rightarrow Base = 40 \div 0.10 = 400$
40 is 10% of 400.

✎ *Solve each problem.*

1) 20 is what percent of 200? ____%

2) 40 is what percent of 50? ____%

3) 30 is 15 percent of what number? ____

4) 18 is 6 percent of what? ____

5) 20 is what percent of 50? ____%

6) 18 is what percent of 90? ____%

7) 25 is what percent of 80? ____%

8) 60 is what percent of 300? ____%

9) 50 is 20 percent of what number? ____

10) 68 *is 16 percent of what?* ____

11) 15 *is 25 percent of what?* ____

12) 80 *is 25 percent of what?* ____

Percent of Increase and Decrease

Step-by-step guide:

To find the percentage of increase or decrease:
- ✓ New Number – Original Number
- ✓ The result ÷ Original Number × 100
- ✓ If your answer is a negative number, then this is a percentage decrease. If it is positive, then this is a percent of increase.

Examples:

1) Increased by 20%, the numbers 30 becomes:

   First find 20% of 30 → $\frac{20}{100} \times 30 = \frac{20 \times 30}{100} = 6$

   Then: $30 + 6 = 36$

2) The price of a shirt increases from \$10 to \$15. What is the percent increase?
   First: $15 - 10 = 5$
   5 is the result. Then: $5 \div 10 = \frac{5}{10} = 0.5 = 50\%$

✎ *Solve each percent of change word problem.*

1) Bob got a raise, and his hourly wage increased from \$20 to \$25. What is the percent increase? _____ %

2) The price of a pair of shoes increases from \$18 to \$27. What is the percent increase? ____ %

3) At a coffeeshop, the price of a cup of coffee increased from \$1.50 to \$1.80. What is the percent increase in the cost of the coffee? _____ %

4) 4 cm are cut from a 20 cm board. What is the percent decrease in length? _____ %

5) In a class, the number of students has been increased from 25 to 29. What is the percent increase? _____ %

6) The price of gasoline rose from \$2.60 to \$2.86 in one month. By what percent did the gas price rise? _____ %

7) A shirt was originally priced at \$48. It went on sale for \$38.40. What was the percent that the shirt was discounted? _____ %

Discount, Tax and Tip

Step-by-step guide:

- ✓ Discount = Multiply the regular price by the rate of discount
- ✓ Selling price = original price – discount
- ✓ Tax: To find tax, multiply the tax rate to the taxable amount (income, property value, etc.)
- ✓ To find tip, multiply the rate to the selling price.

Examples:

1) With an 20% discount, Ella was able to save $40 on a dress. What was the original price of the dress?

$20\% \ of \ x = \ 40, \frac{20}{100} \times x = 40, x = \frac{100 \times 40}{20} = 200$

2) Sophia purchased a sofa for $250.40. The sofa is regularly priced at $313.125. What was the percent discount Sophia received on the sofa?

Use this formula: $percent = Part \div base = 250.50 \div 313.125 = 0.80 = 80\%$

Therefore, the discount is: $100\% - 80\% = 20\%$

✍ *Find the selling price of each item.*

1) Original price of a computer: $200

Tax: 10%, Selling price: $_____

2) Original price of a laptop: $400

Tax: 5%, Selling price: $_____

3) Original price of a sofa: $500

Tax: 8%, Selling price: $_____

4) Original price of a car: $800

Tax: 25%, Selling price: $_____

5) Original price of a Table: $250

Tax: 10%, Selling price: $_____

6) Original price of a house: $1,500

Tax: 15%   Selling price: $_____

7) Original price of a tablet: $600

Discount: 20%, Selling price: $_____

8) Original price of a chair: $450

Discount: 25%, Selling price: $_____

9) Original price of a book: $125

Discount: 15%, Selling price: $_____

10) Original price of a cellphone: $900

Discount: 12%, Selling price: $_____

Answers – Chapter 7

Percentage Calculations

1) 10
2) 20
3) 10
4) 21

5) 9
6) 40
7) 30
8) 9

9) 36
10) 24.94
11) 17.82
12) 79.52

Percent Problems

1) 10%
2) 80%
3) 200
4) 300

5) 40%
6) 20%
7) 31.25%
8) 20%

9) 250%
10) 425
11) 60
12) 320

Percent of Increase and Decrease

1) 25%
2) 50%
3) 20%
4) 20%

5) 16%
6) 10%
7) 20%

Markup, Discount, and Tip

1) $220.00
2) $420.00
3) $540.00
4) $1,000.00
5) $275.00

6) $1,725
7) $480.00
8) $337.50
9) $106.25
10) $792.00

Chapter 8:
Exponents and Variables

Math Topics that you'll learn Chapter:

- ✓ Multiplication Property of Exponents

- ✓ Division Property of Exponents

- ✓ Powers of Products and Quotients

- ✓ Zero and Negative Exponents

- ✓ Negative Exponents and Negative Bases

- ✓ Scientific Notation

- ✓ Square Roots

Mathematics is an art of human understanding. ~ William Thurston

Multiplication Property of Exponents

Step-by-step guide:

- ✓ Exponents are shorthand for repeated multiplication of the same number by itself. For example, instead of 2×2, we can write 2^2. For $3 \times 3 \times 3 \times 3$, we can write 3^4
- ✓ In algebra, a variable is a letter used to stand for a number. The most common letters are: $x, y, z, a, b, c, m,$ and n.
- ✓ Exponent's rules: $x^a \times x^b = x^{a+b}$, $\frac{x^a}{x^b} = x^{a-b}$

$$(x^a)^b = x^{a \times b}, \qquad (xy)^a = x^a \times y^a , (\frac{a}{b})^c = \frac{a^c}{b^c}$$

Examples:

1) Multiply. $4x^3 \times 2x^2 =$

   Use Exponent's rules: $x^a \times x^b = x^{a+b} \rightarrow x^3 \times x^2 = x^{3+2} = x^5$

   Then: $4x^3 \times 2x^2 = 8x^5$

2) Multiply. $(x^3y^5)^2 =$

   Use Exponent's rules: $(x^a)^b = x^{a \times b}$. Then: $(x^3y^5)^2 = x^{3 \times 2}y^{5 \times 2} = x^6y^{10}$

✎ *Simplify and write the answer in exponential form.*

1) $2x^2 \times 4x =$

2) $5x^4 \times x^2 =$

3) $8x^4 \times 3x^5 =$

4) $3x^2 \times 6xy =$

5) $2x^5y \times 4x^2y^3 =$

6) $9x^2y^5 \times 5x^2y^8 =$

7) $5x^2y \times 5x^2y^7 =$

8) $7x^6 \times 3x^9y^4 =$

9) $8x^8y^5 \times 7x^5y^3 =$

10) $9x^6x^2 \times 4xy^5 =$

11) $12xy^7 \times 2x^9y^8 =$

12) $9x^9y^{12} \times 9x^{14}y^{11} =$

Division Property of Exponents

Step-by-step guide:

- ✓ For division of exponents use these formulas: $\frac{x^a}{x^b} = x^{a-b}$, $x \neq 0$

$$\frac{x^a}{x^b} = \frac{1}{x^{b-a}}, x \neq 0, \qquad \frac{1}{x^b} = x^{-b}$$

Examples:

1) Simplify. $\frac{12x^2y}{4xy^3} =$

First cancel the common factor: $4 \rightarrow \frac{12x^2y}{4xy^3} = \frac{3x^2y}{xy^3}$

Use Exponent's rules: $\frac{x^a}{x^b} = x^{a-b} \rightarrow \frac{x^2}{x} = x^{2-1} = x$ and $\frac{y}{y^3} = y^{1-3} = y^{-2}$

Then: $\frac{12x^2y}{4xy^3} = \frac{3x}{y^2}$

2) Divide. $\frac{18x^{-6}}{2x^{-3}} =$

Use Exponent's rules: $\frac{x^a}{x^b} = \frac{1}{x^{b-a}} \rightarrow \frac{x^{-6}}{x^{-3}} = \frac{1}{x^{-3-(-6)}} = \frac{1}{x^{-3+6}} = \frac{1}{x^3}$

Then: $\frac{18x^{-6}}{2x^{-3}} = \frac{9}{x^3}$

✎ *Simplify.*

1) $\frac{5^2 \times 5^3}{5^4 \times 5^2} =$

2) $\frac{4x}{8x^2} =$

3) $\frac{15x^6}{3x^5} =$

4) $\frac{18x^5}{12x^8} =$

5) $\frac{24x^5}{4y^3} =$

6) $\frac{36xy^3}{2x^5y^2} =$

7) $\frac{8x^8y}{3xy^2} =$

8) $\frac{20x^5y^9}{4x^3} =$

9) $\frac{28x^2}{8x^5y^3} =$

10) $\frac{25yx^4}{5yx^8} =$

11) $\frac{45x^4y}{9x^8y^2} =$

12) $\frac{4x^8y^2}{20x^8y} =$

Powers of Products and Quotients

Step-by-step guide:

✓ For any nonzero numbers a and b and any integer x, $(ab)^x = a^x \times b^x$.

Example:

1) Simplify. $(6x^2y^4)^2 =$

Use Exponent's rules: $(x^a)^b = x^{a \times b}$

$(6x^2y^4)^2 = (6)^2(x^2)^2(y^4)^2 = 36x^{2 \times 2}y^{4 \times 2} = 36x^4y^8$

2) Simplify. $(\frac{5x}{2x^2})^2 =$

First cancel the common factor: $x \rightarrow (\frac{5x}{2x^2})^2 = (\frac{5}{2x})^2$

Use Exponent's rules: $(\frac{a}{b})^c = \frac{a^c}{b^c}$

Then: $(\frac{5}{2x})^2 = \frac{5^2}{(2x)^2} = \frac{25}{4x^2}$

✍ *Simplify.*

1) $(x^2y^6)^2 =$

2) $(x^3 \times y)^2 =$

3) $(2x^5y^3)^2 =$

4) $(3x^3y^6)^2 =$

5) $(4x^5y^6)^3 =$

6) $(5x \times 2y^5)^2 =$

7) $(\frac{3x}{x^2})^3 =$

8) $\left(\frac{x^2y^3}{x^2y^2}\right)^3 =$

9) $\left(\frac{16x}{4x^6}\right)^2 =$

10) $\left(\frac{2x^5}{x^2y^2}\right)^2 =$

11) $\left(\frac{xy^2}{x^2y^3}\right)^{-2} =$

12) $\left(\frac{8xy^2}{x^3}\right)^2 =$

Zero and Negative Exponents

Step-by-step guide:

- ✓ A negative exponent simply means that the base is on the wrong side of the fraction line, so you need to flip the base to the other side. For instance, "x^{-2}" (pronounced as "ecks to the minus two") just means "x^2" but underneath, as in $\frac{1}{x^2}$.

Example:

1) Evaluate. $\left(\frac{2}{3}\right)^{-2} =$

Use Exponent's rules: $\frac{1}{x^b} = x^{-b} \rightarrow \left(\frac{2}{3}\right)^{-2} = \frac{1}{\left(\frac{2}{3}\right)^2} = \frac{1}{\frac{2^2}{3^2}}$

Now use fraction rule: $\frac{1}{\frac{b}{c}} = \frac{c}{b} \rightarrow \frac{1}{\frac{2^2}{3^2}} = \frac{3^2}{2^2} = \frac{9}{4}$

2) Evaluate. $\left(\frac{4}{5}\right)^{-3} =$

Use Exponent's rules: $\frac{1}{x^b} = x^{-b} \rightarrow \left(\frac{4}{5}\right)^{-3} = \frac{1}{\left(\frac{4}{5}\right)^3} = \frac{1}{\frac{4^3}{5^3}}$

Now use fraction rule: $\frac{1}{\frac{b}{c}} = \frac{c}{b} \rightarrow \frac{1}{\frac{4^3}{5^3}} = \frac{5^3}{4^3} = \frac{125}{64}$

✍ ***Evaluate the following expressions.***

1) $3^{-2} =$

2) $2^{-3} =$

3) $5^{-3} =$

4) $4^{-3} =$

5) $6^{-3} =$

6) $8^{-2} =$

7) $5^{-4} =$

8) $10^{-2} =$

9) $\left(\frac{1}{5}\right)^{-1}$

10) $\left(\frac{1}{4}\right)^{-2} =$

11) $\left(\frac{1}{5}\right)^{-3} =$

12) $\left(\frac{3}{4}\right)^{-2} =$

Negative Exponents and Negative Bases

Step-by-step guide:

- ✓ Make the power positive. A negative exponent is the reciprocal of that number with a positive exponent.
- ✓ The parenthesis is important!
- ✓ 5^{-2} is not the same as $(-5)^{-2}$

$$(-5)^{-2} = -\frac{1}{5^2} \text{ and } (-5)^{-2} = +\frac{1}{5^2}$$

Example:

1) Simplify. $\left(\frac{5a}{6c}\right)^{-2} =$

Use Exponent's rules: $\frac{1}{x^b} = x^{-b} \rightarrow \left(\frac{5a}{6c}\right)^{-2} = \frac{1}{\left(\frac{5a}{6c}\right)^2} = \frac{1}{\frac{5^2 a^2}{6^2 c^2}}$

Now use fraction rule: $\frac{1}{\frac{b}{c}} = \frac{c}{b} \rightarrow \frac{1}{\frac{5^2 a^2}{6^2 c^2}} = \frac{6^2 c^2}{5^2 a^2}$

Then: $\frac{6^2 c^2}{5^2 a^2} = \frac{36 c^2}{25 a^2}$

2) Simplify. $\left(\frac{2x}{3yz}\right)^{-3} =$

Use Exponent's rules: $\frac{1}{x^b} = x^{-b} \rightarrow \left(\frac{2x}{3yz}\right)^{-3} = \frac{1}{\left(\frac{2x}{3yz}\right)^3} = \frac{1}{\frac{2^3 x^3}{3^3 y^3 z^3}}$

Now use fraction rule: $\frac{1}{\frac{b}{c}} = \frac{c}{b} \rightarrow \frac{1}{\frac{2^3 x^3}{3^3 y^3 z^3}} = \frac{3^3 y^3 z^3}{2^3 x^3} = \frac{27 y^3 z^3}{8 x^3}$

✎ ***Simplify.***

1) $2x^{-2}y^{-3} =$

2) $3x^{-5}y^{-2} =$

3) $6a^{-3}b^{-5} =$

4) $7x^4 y^{-3} =$

5) $-\dfrac{9}{x^{-4}} =$

6) $\dfrac{12b}{-9c^{-5}} =$

7) $\dfrac{16ab}{a^{-2}b^{-3}} =$

8) $\dfrac{15n^{-2}}{20p^{-3}} =$

9) $\dfrac{16ab^{-5}}{4c^{-2}} =$

10) $\left(\dfrac{5x}{2y}\right)^{-2} =$

11) $\left(-\dfrac{2x}{3yz}\right)^{-4} =$

12) $\dfrac{5ab^{-3}}{-3c^{-2}} =$

13) $\left(-\dfrac{x^5}{x^3}\right)^{-2} =$

Scientific Notation

Step-by-step guide:

- ✓ It is used to write very big or very small numbers in decimal form.
- ✓ In scientific notation all numbers are written in the form of:

$$m \times 10^n$$

Decimal notation	Scientific notation
5	5×10^0
– 25,000	-2.5×10^4
0.5	5×10^{-1}
2,122.456	$2,122456 \times 10^{-3}$

Example:

1) Write 0.00015 in scientific notation.

First, move the decimal point to the right so that you have a number that is between 1 and 10. Then: $N = 1.5$

Second, determine how many places the decimal moved in step 1 by the power of 10.

Then: $10^{-4} \rightarrow$ When the decimal moved to the right, the exponent is negative.

Then: $0.00015 = 1.5 \times 10^{-4}$

2) Write 9.5×10^{-5} in standard notation.

$10^{-5} \rightarrow$ When the decimal moved to the right, the exponent is negative.

Then: $9.5 \times 10^{-5} = 0.000095$

 *Write each number in scientific notation.*

1) $15,000,000 =$ 3) $0.000819 =$

2) $67,000 =$ 4) $0.00092 =$

 *Write each number in standard notation.*

5) $4.5 \times 10^3 =$ 7) $6 \times 10^{-1} =$

6) $8 \times 10^{-4} =$ 8) $9 \times 10^{-2} =$

Square Roots

Step-by-step guide:

✓ A square root of x is a number r whose square is: $r^2 = x$

r is a square root of x.

Example:

1) Find the square root of $\sqrt{169}$.

First factor the number: $169 = 13^2$, Then: $\sqrt{169} = \sqrt{13^2}$

Now use radical rule: $\sqrt[n]{a^n} = a$

Then: $\sqrt{13^2} = 13$

2) Evaluate. $\sqrt{9} \times \sqrt{25} =$

First factor the numbers: $9 = 3^2$ and $25 = 5^2$

Then: $\sqrt{9} \times \sqrt{25} = \sqrt{3^2} \times \sqrt{5^2}$

Now use radical rule: $\sqrt[n]{a^n} = a$, Then: $\sqrt{3^2} \times \sqrt{5^2} = 3 \times 5 = 15$

✎ *Evaluate.*

1) $\sqrt{16} \times \sqrt{4} = $ _____

2) $\sqrt{9} \times \sqrt{49} = $ _____

3) $\sqrt{4} \times \sqrt{8} = $ _____

4) $\sqrt{9} \times \sqrt{6} = $ _____

5) $\sqrt{25} \times \sqrt{5} = $ _____

6) $\sqrt{6} \times \sqrt{6} = $ _____

7) $\sqrt{5} + \sqrt{5} = $ _____

8) $\sqrt{12} + \sqrt{12} = $ _____

9) $3\sqrt{6} - 2\sqrt{6} = $ _____

10) $3\sqrt{5} \times 2\sqrt{5} = $ _____

11) $6\sqrt{8} \times 2\sqrt{8} = $ _____

12) $6\sqrt{4} - \sqrt{16} = $ _____

Answers – Chapter 8

Multiplication Property of Exponents

1) $8x^3$
2) $5x^6$
3) $24x^9$
4) $18x^3y$

5) $8x^7y^4$
6) $45x^4y^{13}$
7) $25x^4y^8$
8) $21x^{15}y^4$

9) $56x^{13}y^8$
10) $36x^9y^5$
11) $24x^{10}y^{15}$
12) $81x^{23}y^{23}$

Division Property of Exponents

1) $\frac{1}{5}$
2) $\frac{1}{2x}$
3) $5x$
4) $\frac{3}{2x^3}$

5) $\frac{6x^5}{y^3}$
6) $\frac{18y}{x^4}$
7) $\frac{8x^7}{3y}$
8) $5x^2y^9$

9) $\frac{7}{2x^3y^3}$
10) $\frac{5}{x^4}$
11) $\frac{5}{x^4y}$
12) $\frac{y}{5}$

Powers of Products and Quotients

1) x^4y^{12}
2) x^6y^2
3) $4x^{10}y^6$
4) $9x^6y^{12}$
5) $64x^{15}y^{18}$

6) $100x^2y^{10}$
7) $\frac{27}{x^3}$
8) y^3
9) $\frac{16}{x^{10}}$

10) $\frac{4x^6}{y^4}$
11) x^2y^2
12) $\frac{64y^{10}}{x^4}$

Zero and Negative Exponents

1) $\frac{1}{9}$
2) $\frac{1}{8}$
3) $\frac{1}{125}$
4) $\frac{1}{64}$

5) $\frac{1}{216}$
6) $\frac{1}{64}$
7) $\frac{1}{625}$
8) $\frac{1}{100}$

9) 5
10) 16
11) 125
12) $\frac{16}{9}$

Negative Exponents and Negative Bases

1) $\dfrac{2}{x^2 y^3}$

2) $\dfrac{3}{x^5 y^2}$

3) $\dfrac{6}{a^3 b^5}$

4) $\dfrac{7x^4}{y^3}$

5) $-9x^4$

6) $-\dfrac{4bc^5}{3}$

7) $16a^3 b^4$

8) $\dfrac{3p^3}{4n^2}$

9) $\dfrac{4ac^2}{b^5}$

10) $\dfrac{4y^2}{25x^2}$

11) $\dfrac{81y^4 z^4}{16x^4}$

12) $-\dfrac{5ac^2}{3b^3}$

13) $\dfrac{1}{x^4}$

Scientific Notation

1) 1.5×10^7

2) 6.7×10^4

3) 8.19×10^{-4}

4) 9.2×10^{-4}

5) $4,500$

6) 0.0008

7) 0.6

8) 0.09

Square Roots

1) 8

2) 21

3) $4\sqrt{2}$

4) $3\sqrt{6}$

5) $5\sqrt{5}$

6) 6

7) $2\sqrt{5}$

8) $4\sqrt{3}$

9) $\sqrt{6}$

10) 30

11) 96

12) 8

Chapter 9:
Expressions and Variables

Math Topics that you'll learn Chapter:

- ✓ Simplifying Variable Expressions

- ✓ Simplifying Polynomial Expressions

- ✓ Translate Phrases into an Algebraic Statement

- ✓ The Distributive Property

- ✓ Evaluating One Variable

- ✓ Evaluating Two Variables

- ✓ Combining like Terms

Mathematics is, as it were, a sensuous logic, and relates to philosophy as do the arts, music, and plastic art to poetry. – K.

Shegel

Simplifying Variable Expressions

Step-by-step guide:

- ✓ In algebra, a variable is a letter used to stand for a number. The most common letters are: $x, y, z, a, b, c, m,$ and n.
- ✓ algebraic expression is an expression contains integers, variables, and the math operations such as addition, subtraction, multiplication, division, etc.
- ✓ In an expression, we can combine "like" terms. (values with same variable and same power)

Examples:

1) Simplify this expression. $(2x + 3x + 4) = ?$
   Combine like terms. Then: $(2x + 3x + 4) = 5x + 4$ (remember you cannot combine variables and numbers.
2) Simplify this expression. $12 - 3x^2 + 5x + 4x^2 = ?$
   Combine "like" terms: $-3x^2 + 4x^2 = x^2$

   Then: $= 12 + x^2 + 5x$. Write in standard form (biggest powers first): $x^2 + 5x + 12$

✎ *Simplify each expression.*

1) $x - 4 + 6 - 2x =$

2) $3 - 4x + 14 - 3x =$

3) $33x - 5 + 13 + 4x =$

4) $-3 - x^2 - 7x^2 =$

5) $4 + 11x^2 + 3 =$

6) $7x^2 + 5x + 6x^2 =$

7) $42x + 15 + 3x^2 =$

8) $6x(x - 2) - 5 =$

9) $7x - 6 + 9x + 3x^2 =$

10) $(-5)(7x - 2) + 12x =$

11) $15x - 6(6 - 7x) =$

12) $25x + 6(7x + 2) + 14 =$

Simplifying Polynomial Expressions

Step-by-step guide:

- ✓ In mathematics, a polynomial is an expression consisting of variables and coefficients that involves only the operations of addition, subtraction, multiplication, and non-negative integer exponents of variables.

$$P(x) = a_n x^n + a_{n-1} x^{n-1} + \ldots + a_2 x^2 + a_1 x + a_0$$

Examples:

1) Simplify this Polynomial Expressions. $x^2 - 5x^3 + 2x^4 - 4x^3 =$
   Combine "like" terms: $-5x^3 - 4x^3 = -9x^3$
   Then: $x^2 - 5x^3 + 2x^4 - 4x^3 = x^2 - 9x^3 + 2x^4$
   Then write in standard form: $= 2x^4 - 9x^3 + x^2$

2) Simplify this expression. $(2x^2 - x^3) - (x^3 - 4x^2) =$
   First use distributive property: → multiply $(-)$ into $(x^3 - 4x^2)$
   $(2x^2 - x^3) - (x^3 - 4x^2) = 2x^2 - x^3 - x^3 + 4x^2$
   Then combine "like" terms: $2x^2 - x^3 - x^3 + 4x^2 = 6x^2 - 2x^3$
   And write in standard form: $= -2x^3 + 6x^2$

✎ *Simplify each polynomial.*

1) $4x^2 + 7x^3 - 9x^2 + 15x =$ _____

2) $3x^4 - 6x^5 + 7x^4 - 9x^2 =$ _____

3) $6x^3 + 18x - x^2 - 3x^3 =$ _____

4) $3x^3 - (5x^4 + 3x) + x^2 =$ _____

5) $x^4 - 3(x^2 + x) + 2x =$ _____

6) $(6x^3 - 4) + 3(4x^2 - 2x^3) =$ _____

7) $(5x^3 - 3x) - 3(6x^3 - 4x^4) =$ _____

8) $3(6x - 2x^3) - 4(2x^3 + 3x^2) =$ _____

Translate Phrases into an Algebraic Statement

Step-by-step guide:

Translating key words and phrases into algebraic expressions:

- ✓ Addition: plus, more than, the sum of, etc.
- ✓ Subtraction: minus, less than, decreased, etc.
- ✓ Multiplication: times, product, multiplied, etc.
- ✓ Division: quotient, divided, ratio, etc.

Examples:

Write an algebraic expression for each phrase.

1) 12 times the sum of 5 and x.

Sum of 5 and x: $5 + x$. Times means multiplication. Then: $12 \times (5 + x)$

2) Nine more than a number is 18.

More than mean plus a number $= x$

Then: $9 + x = 18$

✎ *Write an algebraic expression for each phrase.*

1) 9 decreased by y. _____

2) Add y to 16. _____

3) The square of 8. _____

4) 7 multiplied by x. _____

5) Subtract 22 from y. _____

6) 13 divided by x. _____

7) x raised to the fifth power. _____

8) The sum of five and a number. _____

9) The difference between fifty–four and y. _____

10) The quotient of eleven and a number. _____

11) The quotient of the square of b and 8. _____

12) The difference between x and 24 is 18. _____

The Distributive Property

Step-by-step guide:

✓ Distributive Property:
$$a(b + c) = ab + ac$$

Examples:

1) Simply. $(-2)(x - 3) =$

Use Distributive Property formula: $a(b + c) = ab + ac$
$(-2)(x - 3) = -2x + 6$

2) Simply $(5)(6x - 3) =$

Use Distributive Property formula: $a(b + c) = ab + ac$
$(5)(6x - 3) = 30x - 15$

✎ *Use the distributive property to simply each expression.*

1) $(-4)(x - 7) =$

2) $-(8 - 5x) =$

3) $7(7 + 3x) =$

4) $3(14 + 3x) =$

5) $(-7x + 6)3 =$

6) $6(5 + 7x) =$

7) $12(4x + 3) =$

8) $(-3x + 5)5 =$

9) $(5 - 8x)(-9) =$

10) $(-4)(2 - 16x) =$

11) $12(4x - 15) =$

12) $(-15x + 20)(-2) =$

Evaluating One Variable

Step-by-step guide:

- ✓ To evaluate one variable expression, find the variable and substitute a number for that variable.
- ✓ Perform the arithmetic operations.

Examples:

1) Solve this expression. $18 - 2x$, $x = 2$

First substitute 2 for x, then:

$18 - 2x = 18 - 2(2) = 18 - 4 = 14$

2) Solve this expression. $5 - 2x$, $x = -1$

First substitute -1 for x, then:

$5 - 2x = 5 - 2(-1) = 5 + 2 = 7$

✎ *Evaluate each expression using the value given.*

1) $3x - 6$, $x = 3$

2) $6x + 5$, $x = -2$

3) $10 - x$, $x = 2$

4) $x + 3$, $x = 4$

5) $2x + 6$, $x = 7$

6) $12 - 2x$, $x = -3$

7) $4x + 5$, $x = 3$

8) $5x + 7$, $x = -2$

9) $12 + 3x - 7$, $x = 2$

10) $6(5x + 3)$, $x = 7$

11) $3(-6x - 3)$, $x = 4$

12) $8x - 4x + 14$, $x = 5$

Evaluating Two Variables

Step-by-step guide:

✓ To evaluate an algebraic expression, substitute a number for each variable and perform the arithmetic operations.

Examples:

1) Solve this expression. $4(2a - b), a = 2, b = -1$

First substitute 2 for a, and -1 for b , then:

$4(2a - b), 8a - 4b = 8(2) - 4(-1) = 16 + 4 = 20$

2) Solve this expression. $2x + 6y , x = 1, y = 2$

First substitute 1 for x, and 2 for y , then:

$2x + 6y = 2(1) + 6(2) = 2 + 12 = 14$

✎ *Evaluate each expression using the values given.*

1) $x + 2y,$

   $x = 1, y = 2$

2) $2x - 3y,$

   $x = 1, y = -2$

3) $-a + 5b,$

   $a = -2, b = 3$

4) $-3a + 5b,$

   $a = 5, b = 2$

5) $5x + 8 - 3y,$

   $x = 5, y = 4$

6) $3x + 5y,$

   $x = 2, y = 3$

7) $7x + 6y,$

   $x = 2, y = 4$

8) $3a - (12 - b),$

   $a = 3, b = 5$

9) $4z + 20 + 7k,$

   $z = -4, k = 5$

10) $xy + 15 + 4x,$

   $x = 6, y = 3$

11) $8x + 3 - 5y + 4,$

   $x = 6, y = 3$

12) $5 + 2(-3x - 4y),$

   $x = 6, y = 5$

Combining like Terms

Step-by-step guide:

- ✓ Terms are separated by "+" and "-" signs.
- ✓ Like terms are terms with same variables and same powers.
- ✓ Be sure to use the "+" or "-" that is in front of the coefficient.

Examples:

1) Simplify this expression. $(-2)(2x - 2) =$

First use Distributive Property formula: $a(b + c) = ab + ac$
$(-2)(2x - 2) = -4x + 4$

2) Simplify this expression. $4(-2x + 6) =$

Use Distributive Property formula: $a(b + c) = a + ac$
$4(-2x + 6) = -8x + 24$

✎ *Simplify each expression.*

1) $-4x + x + 5 =$

2) $-2(3x - 4) =$

3) $-14x + 6 - 12x =$

4) $8x - 12 - 3x + 3 =$

5) $13x + 5x - 22 =$

6) $3(4x + 8) + 7x =$

7) $3(5 - 2x) - 20x =$

8) $-5x - (7 - 15x) =$

9) $5(-15x + 3) - 17x =$

10) $-8x - 23 + 19x =$

11) $24x - 13x + 8 - 6x =$

12) $(-3)(8x - 5) - 19x =$

Answers – Chapter 9

Simplifying Variable Expressions

1) $-x + 2$
2) $-7x + 17$
3) $37x + 8$
4) $-8x^2 - 3$
5) $11x^2 + 7$
6) $13x^2 + 5x$

7) $3x^2 + 42x + 15$
8) $6x^2 - 12x - 5$
9) $3x^2 + 16x - 6$
10) $-23x + 10$
11) $57x - 36$
12) $67x + 26$

Simplifying Polynomial Expressions

1) $7x^3 - 5x^2 + 15x$
2) $-6x^5 + 10x^4 - 9x^2$
3) $3x^3 - x^2 + 18x$
4) $-5x^4 + 3x^3 + x^2 - 3x$

5) $x^4 - 3x^2 - x$
6) $12x^2 - 4$
7) $12x^4 - 13x^3 - 3x$
8) $-14x^3 - 12x^2 + 18x$

Translate Phrases into an Algebraic Statement

1) $9 - y$
2) $y + 16$
3) 8^2
4) $7x$
5) $y - 22$
6) $\frac{13}{x}$
7) x^5

8) $5 + x$
9) $54 - y$
10) $\frac{11}{x}$
11) $\frac{b^2}{8}$
12) $x - 24 = 18$

The Distributive Property

1) $-4x + 28$
2) $5x - 8$
3) $21x + 49$
4) $9x + 42$
5) $-21x + 18$
6) $42x + 30$

7) $48x + 36$
8) $-15x + 25$
9) $72x - 45$
10) $64x - 8$
11) $48x - 180$
12) $30x - 40$

Evaluating One Variable

1) 3
2) -7
3) 8
4) 7
5) 20

6) 18
7) 17
8) -3
9) 11
10) 228

11) -81 12) 34

Evaluating Two Variables

1) 5 8) 2
2) 8 9) 39
3) 17 10) 57
4) -5 11) 40
5) 21 12) -71
6) 21
7) 38

Combining like Terms

1) $-3x + 5$ 7) $-26x + 15$
2) $-6x + 8$ 8) $10x - 7$
3) $-26x + 6$ 9) $-92x + 15$
4) $5x - 9$ 10) $11x - 23$
5) $18x - 22$ 11) $5x + 8$
6) $19x + 24$ 12) $-43x + 15$

Chapter 10:
Equations and Inequalities

Math Topics that you'll learn Chapter:

✓ One–Step Equations

✓ Multi–Step Equations

✓ Graphing Single–Variable Inequalities

✓ One–Step Inequalities

✓ Multi–Step Inequalities

"Life is a math equation. In order to gain the most, you have to know how to convert negatives into positives."

– Anonymous

One–Step Equations

Step-by-step guide:

✓ The values of two expressions on both sides of an equation are equal. $ax + b = c$

✓ You only need to perform one Math operation in order to solve the one-step equations.

✓ To solve one-step equation, find the inverse (opposite) operation is being performed.

✓ The inverse operations are:
  - Addition and subtraction
  - Multiplication and division

Examples:

1) Solve this equation. $2x = 16, x =?$
   Here, the operation is multiplication (variable x is multiplied by 3) and its inverse operation is division. To solve this equation, divide both sides of equation by 2:
   $$2x = 16 \rightarrow 2x \div 2 = 16 \div 2 \rightarrow x = 8$$

2) Solve this equation. $x + 12 = 0 , x = ?$
   Here, the operation is addition and its inverse operation is subtraction. To solve this equation, subtract 12 from both sides of the equation: $x + 12 - 12 = 0 - 12$
   Then simplify: $x + 12 - 12 = 0 - 12 \rightarrow x = -12$

✍ *Solve each equation.*

1) $14 = -2 + x, x =$ ____

2) $x + 7 = 14, x =$ ____

3) $x - 3 = 15, x =$ ____

4) $6 = 14 + x, x =$ ____

5) $x - 4 = 5, x =$ ____

6) $3 - x = -11, x =$ ____

7) $x - 5 = -15, x =$ ____

8) $x - 14 = 14, x =$ ____

9) $x - 15 = -30, x =$ ____

10) $x - 12 = 34, x =$ ____

11) $9 - x = 5, x =$ ____

12) $x - 16 = 16, x =$ ____

Multi–Step Equations

Step-by-step guide:

   ✓ Combine "like" terms on one side.
   ✓ Bring variables to one side by adding or subtracting.
   ✓ Simplify using the inverse of addition or subtraction.
   ✓ Simplify further by using the inverse of multiplication or division.

Examples:

1) Solve this equation. $-(8 - x) = 6$

   First use Distributive Property: $-(8 - x) = -8 + x$

   Now solve by subtract 6 to both sides of the equation. $-8 + x = 6 \rightarrow -8 + x - 6 = 6 - 6$

   Now simplify: $-14 + x = 0 \rightarrow x = 14$

2) Solve this equation. $2x + 5 = 15 - x$

   First bring variables to one side by adding x to both sides.

   $2x + 5 = 15 - x \rightarrow 3x + 5 = 15$. Now, subtract 15 from both sides:

   $3x + 5 - 15 = 15 - 15 \rightarrow 3x - 10 = 0 \rightarrow 3x = 10$

   Now, divide both sides by 3: $3x = 10 \rightarrow 3x \div 3 = \frac{10}{3} \rightarrow x = \frac{10}{3}$

✎ *Solve each equation.*

1) $-(3 - x) = 7$

2) $3x - 15 = 12$

3) $3x - 3 = 9$

4) $3x - 15 = 6$

5) $-3(5 + x) = 3$

6) $-5(3 + x) = 5$

7) $24 = -(x - 7)$

8) $6(4 - 2x) = 30$

9) $18 - 4x = -9 - x$

10) $14 - 2x = 14 + x$

11) $30 + 15x = -6 + 3x$

12) $18 = (-4x) - 9 + 3$

Graphing Single–Variable Inequalities

Step-by-step guide:

- ✓ Inequality is similar to equations and uses symbols for "less than" (<) and "greater than" (>).
- ✓ To solve inequalities, we need to isolate the variable. (like in equations)
- ✓ To graph an inequality, find the value of the inequality on the number line.
- ✓ For less than or greater than draw open circle on the value of the variable.
- ✓ If there is an equal sign too, then use filled circle.
- ✓ Draw a line to the right or to the left for greater or less than.

Examples:

1) Draw a graph for $x > 4$

Since, the variable is greater than 4, then we need to find 4 and draw an open circle above it. Then, draw a line to the right.

2) Graph this inequality. $x < 5$

✎ *Draw a graph for each*

inequality.

1) $x > 2$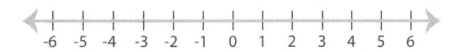

2) $x < -2$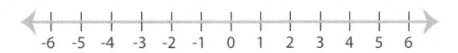

3) $x < 4$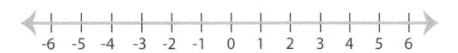

4) $x > -1$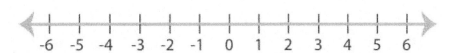

5) $x < 5$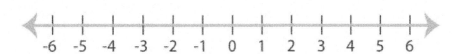

One–Step Inequalities

Step-by-step guide:

✓ Similar to equations, first isolate the variable by using inverse operation.
✓ For dividing or multiplying both sides by negative numbers, flip the direction of the inequality sign.

Examples:

1) Solve and graph the inequality. $x + 2 \geq 3$.

Subtract 2 from both sides. $x + 2 \geq 3 \rightarrow x + 2 - 2 \geq 3 - 2$, then: $x \geq 1$

2) Solve this inequality. $x - 1 \leq 2$

Add 1 to both sides. $x - 1 \leq 2 \rightarrow x - 1 + 1 \leq 2 + 1$, then: $x \leq 3$

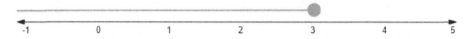

 Solve each inequality and graph it.

1) $4x \geq 8$

2) $2 + x \leq 6$

3) $x + 4 \leq 9$

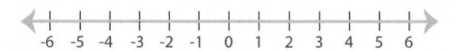

4) $8x \geq 24$

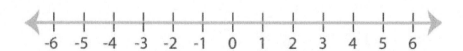

5) $5x \leq 20$

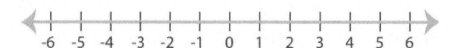

Multi–Step Inequalities

Step-by-step guide:

- ✓ Isolate the variable.
- ✓ Simplify using the inverse of addition or subtraction.
- ✓ Simplify further by using the inverse of multiplication or division.

Examples:

1) Solve this inequality. $x - 2 \leq 4$

First add 2 to both sides: $x - 2 + 2 \leq 4 + 2 \rightarrow x \leq 6$

2) Solve this inequality. $2x + 6 \leq 10$

First add 4 to both sides: $2x + 6 - 6 \leq 10 - 6$

Then simplify: $2x + 6 - 6 \leq 10 - 6 \rightarrow 2x \leq 4$

Now divide both sides by 2: $\frac{2x}{2} \leq \frac{4}{2} \rightarrow x \leq 2$

✏ *Solve each inequality.*

1) $x - 5 \leq 4$

2) $2x - 2 \leq 12$

3) $3 + 2x \leq 11$

4) $x - 6 \geq 12$

5) $3x - 6 \leq 12$

6) $7x - 3 \leq 18$

7) $2x - 3 < 23$

8) $15 - 2x \geq -15$

9) $7 + 3x < 25$

10) $2 + 4x \geq 18$

11) $7 + 3x < 34$

12) $5x - 2 < 8$

Answers – Chapter 10

One–Step Equations

1) 16
2) 7
3) 18
4) −8
5) 9
6) 14

7) −10
8) 28
9) −15
10) 46
11) 4
12) 32

Multi–Step Equations

1) 10
2) 9
3) 4
4) 7
5) −6
6) −4
7) −17

8) $-\frac{1}{2}$
9) 9
10) 0
11) −3
12) −6

Graphing Single–Variable Inequalities

1)

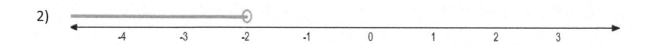

2)

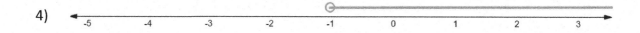

3)

4)

5)

One–Step Inequalities

1)

2)

3)

4)

5)

Multi–Step inequalities

1) $x \leq 9$
2) $x \leq 7$
3) $x \leq 4$
4) $x \geq 18$
5) $x \leq 6$
6) $x \leq 3$
7) $x < 13$
8) $x \leq 15$
9) $x < 6$
10) $x \geq 4$
11) $x < 9$
12) $x < 2$

Chapter 11:
Lines and Slope

Math Topics that you'll learn Chapter:

- ✓ Finding Slope

- ✓ Graphing Lines Using Slope–Intercept Form

- ✓ Graphing Lines Using Standard Form

- ✓ Writing Linear Equations

- ✓ Graphing Linear Inequalities

- ✓ Finding Midpoint

- ✓ Finding Distance of Two Points

"Nature is written in mathematical language." – Galileo Galilei

Finding Slope

Step-by-step guide:

- ✓ The slope of a line represents the direction of a line on the coordinate plane.
- ✓ A coordinate plane contains two perpendicular number lines. The horizontal line is x and the vertical line is y. The point at which the two axes intersect is called the origin. An ordered pair (x, y) shows the location of a point.
- ✓ A line on coordinate plane can be drawn by connecting two points.
- ✓ To find the slope of a line, we need two points.
- ✓ The slope of a line with two points A (x_1, y_1) and B (x_2, y_2) can be found by using this formula: $\frac{y_2 - y_1}{x_2 - x_1} = \frac{rise}{run}$

Examples:

1) Find the slope of the line through these two points: $(1, -9)$ *and* $(2, 5)$.

   Slope $= \frac{y_2 - y_1}{x_2 - x_1}$. Let (x_1, y_1) be $(1, -9)$ and (x_2, y_2) be $(2, 5)$. Then: slope $= \frac{y_2 - y_1}{x_2 - x_1} = \frac{5 - (-9)}{2 - 1} = \frac{5 + 9}{1} = \frac{14}{1} = 14$

2) Find the slope of the line containing two points $(6, 1)$ and $(-2, 9)$.

   Slope $= \frac{y_2 - y_1}{x_2 - x_1} \rightarrow (x_1, y_1) = (6, 1)$ and $(x_2, y_2) = (-2, 9)$. Then: slope $= \frac{y_2 - y_1}{x_2 - x_1} = \frac{9 - 1}{-2 - 6} = \frac{8}{-8} = \frac{1}{-1} = -1$

✎ *Find the slope of the line through each pair of points.*

1) $(7, 4), (5, -2)$

2) $(1, 1), (3, 5)$

3) $(5, 1), (2, 4)$

4) $(-3, 1), (-2, 4)$

5) $(-1, 2), (2, -2)$

6) $(-1, 2), (0, 3)$

7) $(5, -1), (-1, 2)$

8) $(-2, -1), (0, 5)$

9) $(3, 2), (5, 4)$

10) $(5, -4), (2, -1)$

11) $(2, -9), (1, -8)$

12) $(7, -2), (5, 0)$

Graphing Lines Using Slope–Intercept Form

Step-by-step guide:

✓ Slope–intercept form of a line: given the slope m and the y-intercept (the intersection of the line and y-axis) b, then the equation of the line is:
$$y = mx + b$$

Example: *Sketch the graph of* $y = 6x - 1$.

To graph this line, we need to find two points. When x is zero the value of y is -1. And when y is zero the value of x is $\frac{1}{6}$. $x = 0 \rightarrow y = 6(0) - 1 = -1$, $y = 0 \rightarrow 0 = 6x - 1 \rightarrow x = \frac{1}{6}$

Now, we have two points: $(0, -1)$ and $(\frac{1}{6}, 0)$. Find the points and graph the line. Remember that the slope of the line is 6.

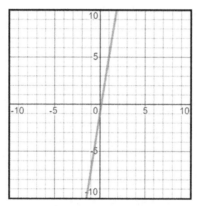

✎ ***Sketch the graph of each line.***

1) $y = x + 4$

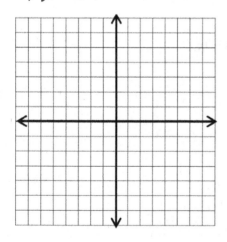

2) $y = 2x - 1$

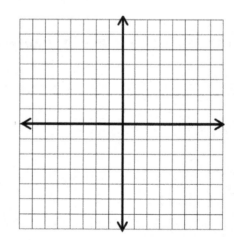

Graphing Lines Using Standard Form

Step-by-step guide:

- ✓ Find the x-intercept of the line by putting zero for y.
- ✓ Find the y-intercept of the line by putting zero for the x.
- ✓ Connect these two points.

Example:

Sketch the graph of $x - y = -2$.

First isolate y for x: $x - y = -2 \rightarrow y = x + 2$

Find the x-intercept of the line by putting zero for y.
$y = x + 2 \rightarrow x + 2 = 0 \rightarrow x = -2$

Find the y-intercept of the line by putting zero for the x.
$y = 0 + 2 \rightarrow y = 2$

Then: x-intercept: $(-2,0)$ and y-intercept: $(0,2)$

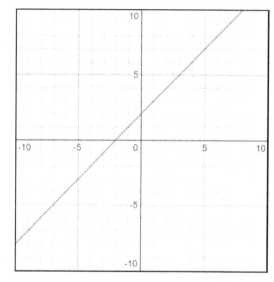

✎ ***Sketch the graph of each line.***

1) $y = -x - 2$ 2) $y = x + 3$ 3) $x + y = -1$

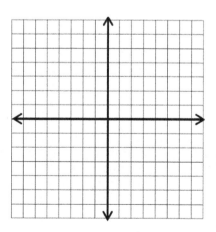 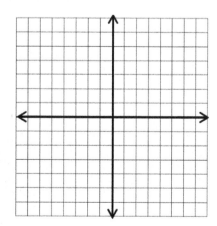 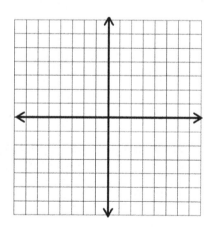

Writing Linear Equations

Step-by-step guide:

- ✓ The equation of a line: $y = mx + b$
- ✓ Identify the slope.
- ✓ Find the y-intercept. This can be done by substituting the slope and the coordinates of a point (x, y) on the line.

Example:

1) What is the equation of the line that passes through $(1, -2)$ and has a slope of 6?

   The general slope-intercept form of the equation of a line is $y = mx + b$, where m is the slope and b is the y-intercept.

   By substitution of the given point and given slope, we have: $-2 = (1)(6) + b$

   So, $b = -2 - 6 = -8$, and the required equation is $y = 6x - 8$.

2) Write the equation of the line through $(1, 1)$ and $(-1, 3)$.

   $Slop = \frac{y_2 - y_1}{x_2 - x_1} = \frac{3 - 1}{-1 - 1} = \frac{2}{-2} = -1 \rightarrow m = -1$

   To find the value of b, you can use either points. The answer will be the same: $y = -x + b$

   $(1, 1) \rightarrow 1 = -1 + b \rightarrow b = 2$

   $(-1, 3) \rightarrow 3 = -(-1) + b \rightarrow b = 2$

   The equation of the line is: $y = -x + 2$

✍ ***Write the equation of the line through the given points.***

1) through: $(2, 4), (1, 2)$

2) through: $(-3, 1), (1, 5)$

3) through: $(-2, 1), (1, 7)$

4) through: $(4, 3), (2, 1)$

5) through: $(-4, 5), (-3, 2)$

6) through: $(8, 3), (7, 2)$

7) through: $(3, -3), (1, 5)$

8) through: $(1, 7), (-4, -3)$

Graphing Linear Inequalities

Step-by-step guide:

- ✓ First, graph the "equals" line.
- ✓ Choose a testing point. (it can be any point on both sides of the line.)
- ✓ Put the value of (x, y) of that point in the inequality. If that works, that part of the line is the solution. If the values don't work, then the other part of the line is the solution.

Example:

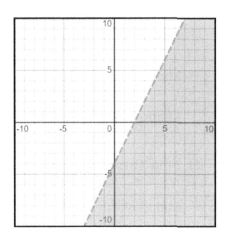

Sketch the graph of $y < 2x - 4$. First, graph the line:

$y = 2x - 4$. The slope is 2 and y-intercept is -4. Then, choose a testing point. The easiest point to test is the origin: $(0, 0)$

$$(0,0) \rightarrow y < 2x - 4 \rightarrow 0 < 2(0) - 4 \rightarrow 0 < -4$$

0 is not less than -4. So, the other part of the line (on the right side) is the solution.

✍ *Sketch the graph of each linear inequality.*

1) $y > 2x - 1$ 　　　　　 2) $y < -2x + 1$ 　　　　　 3) $y \leq -3x + 4$

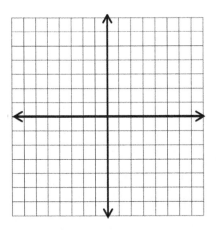 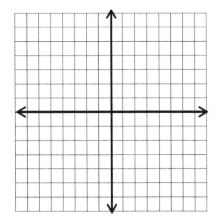 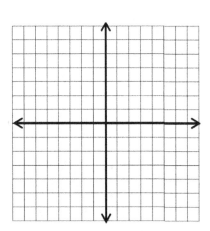

Finding Midpoint

Step-by-step guide:

✓ The middle of a line segment is its midpoint.
✓ The Midpoint of two endpoints A (x_1, y_1) and B (x_2, y_2) can be found using this formula: $M\left(\frac{x_1+x_2}{2}, \frac{y_1+y_2}{2}\right)$

Example:

1) Find the midpoint of the line segment with the given endpoints. $(1, -2), (3, 6)$

Midpoint = $\left(\frac{x_1+x_2}{2}, \frac{y_1+y_2}{2}\right) \rightarrow (x_1, y_1) = (1, -2)$ and $(x_2, y_2) = (3, 6)$

Midpoint = $\left(\frac{1+3}{2}, \frac{-2+6}{2}\right) \rightarrow \left(\frac{4}{2}, \frac{4}{2}\right) \rightarrow M(2, 2)$

2) Find the midpoint of the line segment with the given endpoints. $(-2, 5), (8, -3)$

Midpoint = $\left(\frac{x_1+x_2}{2}, \frac{y_1+y_2}{2}\right) \rightarrow (x_1, y_1) = (-2, 5)$ and $(x_2, y_2) = (8, -3)$

Midpoint = $\left(\frac{-2+8}{2}, \frac{5-3}{2}\right) \rightarrow \left(\frac{6}{2}, \frac{2}{2}\right) \rightarrow M(3, 1)$

✍ *Find the midpoint of the line segment with the given endpoints.*

1) $(2, -1), (0, 3)$

2) $(6, 1), (-2, 5)$

3) $(4, -1), (0, 3)$

4) $(3, 7), (-1, 3)$

5) $(-3, 2), (9, -6)$

6) $(-2, 3), (2, -3)$

7) $(8, 0), (-6, 4)$

8) $(-1, 4), (-3, 0)$

9) $(4, 7), (-2, 5)$

10) $(9, 3), (-3, -7)$

11) $(3, 4), (-9, -6)$

12) $(-2, 8), (-6, -2)$

Finding Distance of Two Points

Step-by-step guide:

✓ Distance of two points A (x_1, y_1) and B (x_2, y_2): $d = \sqrt{(x_2 - x_1)^2 + (y_2 - y_1)^2}$

Example:

1) Find the distance between of $(1, 6), (4, 2)$.

Use distance of two points formula: $d = \sqrt{(x_2 - x_1)^2 + (y_2 - y_1)^2}$

$(x_1, y_1) = (1, 6)$ and $(x_2, y_2) = (4, 2)$. Then: $d = \sqrt{(x_2 - x_1)^2 + (y_2 - y_1)^2} \rightarrow$

$d = \sqrt{(4 - (1))^2 + (2 - 6)^2} = \sqrt{(3)^2 + (-4)^2} = \sqrt{9 + 16} = \sqrt{25} = 5 \rightarrow d = 5$

2) Find the distance of two points $(-1, 5)$ and $(-3, -6)$.

Use distance of two points formula: $d = \sqrt{(x_2 - x_1)^2 + (y_2 - y_1)^2}$

$(x_1, y_1) = (-1, 5)$, and $(x_2, y_2) = (-3, -6)$

Then: $d = \sqrt{(x_2 - x_1)^2 + (y_2 - y_1)^2} \rightarrow d = \sqrt{(-3 - (-1))^2 + (-6 - (5))^2} =$

$\sqrt{(-2)^2 + (-11)^2} = \sqrt{4 + 121} = \sqrt{125} = 5\sqrt{5}$. Then: $d = 5\sqrt{5}$

✎ *Find the distance between each pair of points.*

1) $(-6, 0), (-2, 3)$

2) $(4, 2), (-2, -6)$

3) $(-4, -2), (4, 4)$

4) $(-6, -10), (-2, -10)$

5) $(-1, 1), (-6, -7)$

6) $(3, 2), (8, 2)$

7) $(8, 4), (3, -8)$

8) $(4, 4), (12, 19)$

9) $(-5, 10), (7, 1)$

10) $(7, 7), (-9, -5)$

11) $(9, -3), (3, -11)$

12) $(1, 0), (6, 12)$

Answers – Chapter 11

Finding Slope

1) 3
2) 2
3) −1
4) 3
5) $-\frac{4}{3}$
6) 1

7) $-\frac{1}{2}$
8) 3
9) 1
10) −1
11) −1
12) −1

Graphing Lines Using Slope–Intercept Form

1)

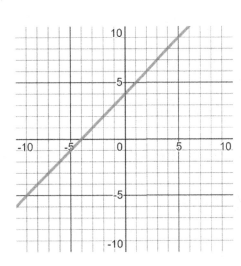

2)

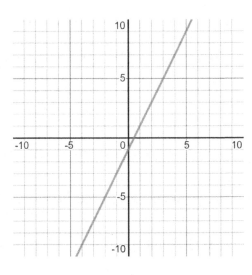

Graphing Lines Using Standard Form

1)

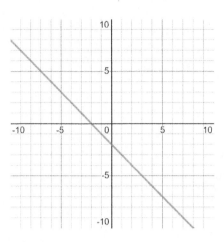

2)

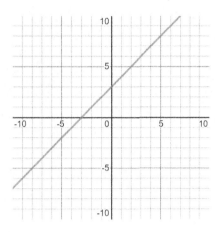

3)

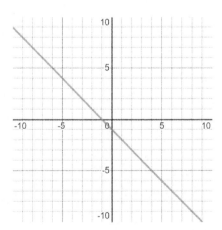

Writing Linear Equations

1) $y = 2x$

2) $y = x + 4$

3) $y = 2x + 5$

4) $y = x - 1$

5) $y = -3x - 7$

6) $y = x - 5$

7) $y = -4x + 9$

8) $y = 2x + 5$

Graphing Linear Inequalities

1)

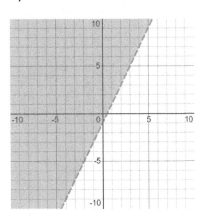

2)

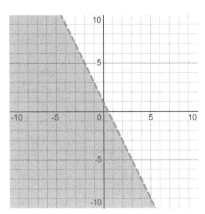

3)

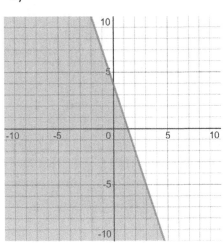

Finding Midpoint

1) $(1, 1)$ 5) $(3, -2)$ 9) $(1, 6)$

2) $(2, 3)$ 6) $(0, 0)$ 10) $(3, -2)$

3) $(2, 1)$ 7) $(1, 2)$ 11) $(-3, -1)$

4) $(1, 5)$ 8) $(-2, 2)$ 12) $(-4, 3)$

Finding Distance of Two Points

1) 5   5) 9.4   9) 15

2) 10   6) 5   10) 20

3) 10   7) 13   11) 10

4) 4   8) 17   12) 13

Chapter 12:
Polynomials

Math Topics that you'll learn Chapter:

- ✓ Writing Polynomials in Standard Form

- ✓ Simplifying Polynomials

- ✓ Adding and Subtracting Polynomials

- ✓ Multiplying Monomials

- ✓ Multiplying and Dividing Monomials

- ✓ Multiplying a Polynomial and a Monomial

- ✓ Multiplying Binomials

- ✓ Factoring Trinomials

- ✓ Operations with Polynomials

Mathematics is the supreme judge; from its decisions there is no appeal. – Tobias Dantzig

Writing Polynomials in Standard Form

Step-by-step guide:

- ✓ A polynomial function $f(x)$ of degree n is of the form
$$f(x) = a_n x^n + a_{n-1} x_{n-1} + \cdots + a_1 x + a_0$$
- ✓ The first term is the one with the biggest power!

Example:

1) Write this polynomial in standard form. $8 + 5x^2 - 3x^3 =$

The first term is the one with the biggest power: $8 + 5x^2 - 3x^3 = -3x^3 + 5x^2 + 8$

2) Write this polynomial in standard form. $5x^2 - 9x^5 + 8x^3 - 11 =$

The first term is the one with the biggest power: $5x^2 - 9x^5 + 8x^3 - 11 =$
$-9x^5 + 8x^3 + 5x^2 - 11$

✎ *Write each polynomial in standard form.*

1) $2x - 5x =$

2) $5 + 12x - 8x =$

3) $x^2 - 2x^3 + 1 =$

4) $2 + 2x^2 - 1 =$

5) $-x^2 + 4x - 2x^3 =$

6) $-2x^2 + 2x^3 + 12 =$

7) $18 - 5x + 9x^4 =$

8) $2x^2 + 13x - 2x^3 =$

9) $8 + 4x^2 - x^3 =$

10) $2x + 3x^3 - 2x^2 =$

11) $-4x^2 + 4x - 6x^3 =$

12) $-3x^2 + 2 - 5x =$

Simplifying Polynomials

Step-by-step guide:

✓ Find "like" terms. (they have same variables with same power).

✓ Use "FOIL". (First-Out-In-Last) for binomials:

$$(x + a)(x + b) = x^2 + (b + a)x + ab$$

✓ Add or Subtract "like" terms using order of operation.

Example:

1) Simplify this expression. $2x(2x - 4) =$

   Use Distributive Property: $2x(2x - 4) = 4x^2 - 8x$

2) Simplify this expression. $(x + 2)(x - 5) =$

   First apply FOIL method: $(a + b)(c + d) = ac + ad + bc + bd$

   $(x + 2)(x - 5) = x^2 - 5x + 2x - 10$

   Now combine like terms: $x^2 - 5x + 2x - 10 = x^2 - 3x - 10$

✍ Simplify each expression.

1) $2(4x - 6) =$

2) $5(3x - 4) =$

3) $x(2x - 5) =$

4) $4(5x + 3) =$

5) $2x(6x - 2) =$

6) $x(3x + 8) =$

7) $(x - 2)(x + 4) =$

8) $(x + 3)(x + 2) =$

9) $(x - 4)(x - 7) =$

10) $(2x + 4)(2x - 5) =$

11) $(4x - 3)(x - 6) =$

12) $(3x + 5)(2x + 4) =$

Adding and Subtracting Polynomials

Step-by-step guide:

✓ Adding polynomials is just a matter of combining like terms, with some order of operations considerations thrown in.
✓ Be careful with the minus signs, and don't confuse addition and multiplication!

Example:

1) Simplify the expressions. $(2x^3 - 4x^4) - (2x^4 - 6x^3) =$

First use Distributive Property for $-(2x^4 - 6x^3) = -2x^4 + 6x^3$

$(2x^3 - 4x^4) - (2x^4 - 6x^3) = 2x^3 - 4x^4 - 2x^4 + 6x^3$

Now combine like terms: $2x^3 - 4x^4 - 2x^4 + 6x^3 = -6x^4 + 8x^3$

2) Add expressions. $(x^3 - 2) + (5x^3 - 3x^2) =$

Remove parentheses: $(x^3 - 2) + (5x^3 - 3x^2) = x^3 - 2 + 5x^3 - 3x^2$

Now combine like terms: $x^3 - 2 + 5x^3 - 3x^2 = 6x^3 - 3x^2 - 2$

✎ *Add or subtract expressions.*

1) $(x^2 - x) + (3x^2 - 5x) =$

2) $(x^3 + 2x) - (3x^3 + 2) =$

3) $(2x^3 - 4) + (2x^3 - 2) =$

4) $(-x^2 - 2) + (2x^2 + 1) =$

5) $(4x^2 + 3) - (3 - 3x^2) =$

6) $(x^3 + 3x^2) - (x^3 - 8) =$

7) $(7x - 9) + (3x + 5) =$

8) $(x^4 - 2x) - (x - x^4) =$

9) $(2x - 4x^3) - (2x^3 + 3x) =$

10) $(x^3 + 5) - (5 - 2x^3) =$

11) $(3x^2 + 2x^3) - (4x^3 + 5) =$

12) $(6x^2 - x) + (2x - 5x^2) =$

Multiplying Monomials

Step-by-step guide:

   ✓ A monomial is a polynomial with just one term, like $2x$ or $7y$.

Example:

1) Multiply expressions. $-2xy^4z^2 \times 4x^2y^5z^3 =$

   Use this formula: $x^a \times x^b = x^{a+b}$

   $x \times x^2 = x^{1+2} = x^3$, $y^4 \times y^5 = y^{4+5} = y^9$ and $z^2 \times z^3 = z^{2+3} = z^5$

   Then: $-2xy^4z^2 \times 4x^2y^5z^3 = -8x^3y^9z^5$

2) Multiply expressions. $-4a^4b^3 \times 5a^3b^2 =$

   Use this formula: $x^a \times x^b = x^{a+b}$

   $a^4 \times a^3 = a^{4+3} = a^7$ and $b^3 \times b^2 = b^{3+2} = b^5$

   Then: $-4a^4b^3 \times 5a^3b^2 = -20a^7b^5$

✎ *Simplify each expression.*

1) $(-2x^4) \times (-5x^3) =$

2) $8x^8 \times -2x^2 =$

3) $5xy^4 \times 2x^2 =$

4) $-2x^6y \times 8xy =$

5) $3x^5 \times (-4x^3y^5) =$

6) $9x^3y^2 \times 3x^2y =$

7) $7xy^4 \times 8x^3y^5 =$

8) $(-5x^2y^4) \times (-2xy^3) =$

9) $9x^5y^2 \times 5x^6y^3 =$

10) $12x^5y^2 \times 2x^3y^3 =$

11) $11x^4y^3z \times 3x^5z^2 =$

12) $20x^5y^8 \times 3x^2y^4 =$

Multiplying and Dividing Monomials

Step-by-step guide:

- ✓ When you divide two monomials you need to divide their coefficients and then divide their variables.
- ✓ In case of exponents with the same base, you need to subtract their powers.
- ✓ Exponent's rules:

$$x^a \times x^b = x^{a+b}, \qquad \frac{x^a}{x^b} = x^{a-b}$$

$$\frac{1}{x^b} = x^{-b}, \quad (x^a)^b = x^{a \times b}$$

$$(xy)^a = x^a \times y^a$$

Example:

1) Multiply expressions. $(8x^5)(-2x^4) =$
   Use this formula: $x^a \times x^b = x^{a+b} \rightarrow x^5 \times x^4 = x^9$
   Then: $(8x^5)(-2x^4) = -16x^9$

2) Dividing expressions. $\frac{-12x^4y^3}{2xy^2} =$
   Use this formula: $\frac{x^a}{x^b} = x^{a-b}$, $\frac{x^4}{x} = x^{4-1} = x^3$ and $\frac{y^3}{y^2} = y$
   Then: $\frac{-12x^4y^3}{2xy^2} = -6x^3y$

✎ *Simplify each expression.*

1) $(x^2y)(xy^2) =$

2) $(x^4y^2)(2x^5y) =$

3) $(-2x^2y)(4x^4y^3) =$

4) $(-3x^5y^2)(2x^2y^4) =$

5) $(-4x^5y^3)(-2x^3y^4) =$

6) $(6x^6y^5)(3x^3y^8) =$

7) $\frac{-2x^4y^3}{x^2y^2} =$

8) $\frac{8x^4y^7}{2x^3y^4} =$

9) $\frac{25x^6y^5}{5x^3y^2} =$

10) $\frac{18x^{12}y^{14}}{6x^8y^6} =$

11) $\frac{45x^{13}y^{15}}{9x^9y^4} =$

12) $\frac{-60x^{20}y^{16}}{3x^{11}y^{13}} =$

Multiplying a Polynomial and a Monomial

Step-by-step guide:

✓ When multiplying monomials, use the product rule for exponents.

✓ When multiplying a monomial by a polynomial, use the distributive property.

$$a \times (b + c) = a \times b + a \times c$$

Example:

1) Multiply expressions. $2x(-2x + 4) =$

Use Distributive Property: $2x(-2x + 4) = -4x^2 + 8x$

2) Multiply expressions. $-2x(3x^2 + 4y^2) =$

Use Distributive Property: $-2x(3x^2 + 4y^2) = -6x^3 - 8xy^2$

✎ *Find each product.*

1) $-2x(5x + 2y) =$

2) $3x(2x - y) =$

3) $4x(x + 5y) =$

4) $-4x(6x - 3) =$

5) $x(-2x + 9y) =$

6) $2x(5x - 8y) =$

7) $x(2x + 4y - 3) =$

8) $2x(x^2 - 2y^2) =$

9) $-4x(2x + 4y) =$

10) $3(x^2 + 7y^2) =$

11) $4x(-x^2y + 2y) =$

12) $5(x^2 - 4xy + 6) =$

Multiplying Binomials

Step-by-step guide:

✓ Use "FOIL". (First-Out-In-Last)
$$(x + a)(x + b) = x^2 + (b + a)x + ab$$

Example:

1) Multiply Binomials. $(x + 3)(x - 2) =$

Use "FOIL". (First–Out–In–Last): $(x + 3)(x - 2) = x^2 - 2x + 3x - 6$

Then simplify: $x^2 - 2x + 3x - 6 = x^2 + x - 6$

2) Multiply Binomials. $(x - 4)(x - 2) =$

Use "FOIL". (First–Out–In–Last):

$(x - 4)(x - 2) = x^2 - 2x - 4x + 8$

Then simplify: $x^2 - 6x + 8 =$

✎ *Find each product.*

1) $(x - 2)(x + 4) =$

2) $(x + 5)(x - 2) =$

3) $(x - 3)(x - 4) =$

4) $(x + 2)(x + 2) =$

5) $(x - 6)(x - 3) =$

6) $(x + 5)(x + 7) =$

7) $(x + 2)(x - 8) =$

8) $(x - 9)(x + 4) =$

9) $(x + 5)(x + 6) =$

10) $(x - 8)(x + 3) =$

11) $(x + 5)(x + 5) =$

12) $(x + 7)(x + 4) =$

Factoring Trinomials

Step-by-step guide:

- ✓ "FOIL":
$$(x + a)(x + b) = x^2 + (b + a)x + ab$$
- ✓ "Difference of Squares":
$$a^2 - b^2 = (a + b)(a - b)$$
$$a^2 + 2ab + b^2 = (a + b)(a + b)$$
$$a^2 - 2ab + b^2 = (a - b)(a - b)$$
- ✓ "Reverse FOIL":
$$x^2 + (b + a)x + ab = (x + a)(x + b)$$

Example:

1) Factor this trinomial. $x^2 - 3x - 18 =$
   Break the expression into groups: $(x^2 + 3x) + (-6x - 18)$
   Now factor out x from $x^2 + 3x : x(x + 2)$, and factor out -6 from $-6x + 18$: $-6(x + 3)$
   Then: $= x(x + 3) - 6(x + 3)$, now factor out like term: $x + 3$
   Then: $(x + 3)(x - 6)$

2) Factor this trinomial. $x^2 + x - 20 =$
   Break the expression into groups: $(x^2 - 4x) + (5x - 20)$
   Now factor out x from $x^2 - 4x : x(x + 3)$, and factor out 5 from $6x - 18$: $5(x - 4)$
   Then: $= x(x - 4) + 5(x - 4)$, now factor out like term: $x - 4$
   Then: $(x + 5)(x - 4)$

✍ *Factor each trinomial.*

1) $x^2 + 3x - 10 =$

2) $x^2 - x - 6 =$

3) $x^2 + 8x + 15 =$

4) $x^2 - 7x + 12 =$

5) $x^2 - x - 20 =$

6) $x^2 + 11x + 18 =$

7) $x^2 + 3x - 28 =$

8) $x^2 - 2x - 48 =$

9) $x^2 - 13x + 36 =$

10) $x^2 - x - 56 =$

11) $x^2 - 4x - 45 =$

12) $x^2 - 8x - 48 =$

Operations with Polynomials

Step-by-step guide:

✓ When multiplying a monomial by a polynomial, use the distributive property.

$$a \times (b + c) = a \times b + a \times c$$

Example:

1) Multiply. $4(3x - 5) =$

Use the distributive property: $4(3x - 5) = 12x - 20$

2) Multiply. $6x(3x + 7) =$

Use the distributive property: $6x(3x + 7) = 18x^2 + 42x$

✐ *Find each product.*

1) $2(3x + 2) =$

2) $-3(2x + 5) =$

3) $4(7x - 3) =$

4) $5(2x - 4) =$

5) $3x(2x - 7) =$

6) $x^2(3x + 4) =$

7) $x^3(x + 5) =$

8) $x^4(5x - 3) =$

9) $4(2x^2 + 3x - 2) =$

10) $-2(x^2 - 6x + 5) =$

11) $5(2x^2 + 4x - 6) =$

12) $-x(3x^2 + 7x + 5) =$

Answers – Chapter 12

Writing Polynomials in Standard Form

1) $-3x$
2) $4x + 5$
3) $-2x^3 + x^2 + 1$
4) $2x^2 + 1$

5) $-2x^3 - x^2 + 4x$
6) $2x^3 - 2x^2 + 12$
7) $9x^4 - 5x + 18$
8) $-2x^3 + 2x^2 + 13x$

9) $-x^3 + 4x^2 + 8$
10) $3x^3 - 2x^2 + 2x$
11) $-6x^3 - 4x^2 + 4x$
12) $-3x^2 - 5x + 2$

Simplifying Polynomials

1) $8x - 12$
2) $15x - 20$
3) $2x^2 - 5x$
4) $20x + 12$

5) $12x^2 - 4x$
6) $3x^2 + 8x$
7) $x^2 + 2x - 8$
8) $x^2 + 5x + 6$

9) $x^2 - 11x + 28$
10) $4x^2 - 2x - 20$
11) $4x^2 - 27x + 18$
12) $6x^2 + 22x + 20$

Adding and Subtracting Polynomials

1) $4x^2 - 6x$
2) $-2x^3 + 2x - 2$
3) $4x^3 - 6$
4) $x^2 - 1$

5) $7x^2$
6) $3x^2 + 8$
7) $10x - 4$
8) $2x^4 - 3x$

9) $-6x^3 - 3x$
10) $3x^3$
11) $-2x^3 + 3x^2 - 5$
12) $x^2 + x$

Multiplying Monomials

1) $10x^7$
2) $-16x^{10}$
3) $10x^3y^4$
4) $-16x^7y^2$

5) $-12x^8y^5$
6) $27x^5y^3$
7) $56x^4y^9$
8) $10x^3y^7$

9) $45x^{11}y^5$
10) $24x^8y^5$
11) $33x^9y^3z^3$
12) $60x^7y^{12}$

Multiplying and Dividing Monomials

1) x^3y^3

2) $2x^9y^3$

3) $-8x^6y^4$

4) $-6x^7y^6$

5) $8x^8y^7$

6) $18x^9y^{13}$

7) $-2x^2y$

8) $4xy^3$

9) $5x^3y^3$

10) $3x^4y^8$

11) $5x^4y^{11}$

12) $-20x^9y^3$

Multiplying a Polynomial and a Monomial

1) $-10x^2 - 4xy$

2) $6x^2 - 3xy$

3) $4x^2 + 20xy$

4) $-24x^2 + 12x$

5) $-2x^2 + 9xy$

6) $10x^2 - 16xy$

7) $2x^2 + 4xy - 3x$

8) $2x^3 - 4xy^2$

9) $-8x^2 - 16xy$

10) $3x^2 + 21y^2$

11) $-4x^3y + 8xy$

12) $5x^2 - 20xy + 30$

Multiplying Binomials

1) $x^2 + 2x - 8$

2) $x^2 + 3x - 10$

3) $x^2 - 7x + 12$

4) $x^2 + 4x + 4$

5) $x^2 - 9x + 18$

6) $x^2 + 12x + 35$

7) $x^2 - 6x - 16$

8) $x^2 - 5x - 36$

9) $x^2 + 11x + 30$

10) $x^2 - 5x - 24$

11) $x^2 + 10x + 25$

12) $x^2 + 11x + 28$

Factoring Trinomials

1) $(x - 2)(x + 5)$

2) $(x + 2)(x - 3)$

3) $(x + 5)(x + 3)$

4) $(x - 3)(x - 4)$

5) $(x - 5)(x + 4)$

6) $(x + 2)(x + 9)$

7) $(x + 7)(x - 4)$

8) $(x - 8)(x + 6)$

9) $(x - 4)(x - 9)$

10) $(x - 8)(x + 7)$

11) $(x - 9)(x + 5)$

12) $(x + 4)(x - 12)$

Operations with Polynomials

1) $6x + 4$

2) $-6x - 15$

3) $28x - 12$

4) $10x - 20$

5) $6x^2 - 21x$

6) $3x^3 + 4x^2$

7) $x^4 + 5x^3$

8) $5x^5 - 3x^4$

9) $8x^2 + 12x - 8$

10) $-2x^2 + 12x - 10$

11) $10x^2 + 20x - 30$

12) $-3x^3 - 7x^2 - 5x$

Chapter 13:
System of Equations

Math Topics that you'll learn Chapter:

- ✓ Solving Systems of Equations

- ✓ Systems of Equations Word Problems

Mathematics is a hard thing to love. It has the unfortunate habit, like a rude dog, of turning its most unfavorable side towards you when you first make contact with it. ~ David Whiteland

Systems of Equations

Step-by-step guide:

- ✓ A system of equations contains two equations and two variables. For example, consider the system of equations: $x - y = 1, x + y = 5$
- ✓ The easiest way to solve a system of equation is using the elimination method. The elimination method uses the addition property of equality. You can add the same value to each side of an equation.
- ✓ For the first equation above, you can add $x + y$ to the left side and 5 to the right side of the first equation: $x - y + (x + y) = 1 + 5$. Now, if you simplify, you get: $x - y + (x + y) = 1 + 5 \rightarrow 2x = 6 \rightarrow x = 3$. Now, substitute 3 for the x in the first equation: $3 - y = 1$. By solving this equation, $y = 2$

Example:

What is the value of $x + y$ in this system of equations? $\begin{cases} 2x + 5y = 11 \\ 4x - 2y = -26 \end{cases}$

Solving Systems of Equations by Elimination

Multiply the first equation by (-2), then add it to the second equation.

$\dfrac{-2(2x + 5y = 11)}{4x - 2y = -26} \Rightarrow \dfrac{-4x - 10y = -22}{4x - 2y = -26} \Rightarrow -12y = -48 \Rightarrow y = 4$

Plug in the value of y into one of the equations and solve for x.

$2x + 5(4) = 11 \Rightarrow 2x + 20 = 11 \Rightarrow 2x = -9 \Rightarrow x = -4.5$

Thus, $x + y = -4.5 + 4 = -0.5$

✎ *Solve each system of equations.*

1) $-4x - 6y = 7$ $x = $ ___

   $x - 2y = 7$ $y = $ ___

2) $-5x + y = -3$ $x = $ ___

   $3x - 7y = 21$ $y = $ ___

3) $3y = -6x + 12$ $x = $ ___

   $8x - 9y = -10$ $y = $ ___

4) $x + 15y = 50$ $x = $ ___

   $x + 10y = 40$ $y = $ ___

5) $3x - 2y = 15$ $x = $ ___

   $3x - 5y = 15$ $y = $ ___

6) $3x - 6y = -12$ $x = $ ___

   $-x - 3y = -6$ $y = $ ___

Systems of Equations Word Problems

Step-by-step guide:

✓ Define your variables, write two equations, and use elimination method for solving systems of equations.

Example:

Tickets to a movie cost $8 for adults and $5 for students. A group of friends purchased **20** tickets for $115.00. How many adults ticket did they buy? ____

Let x be the number of adult tickets and y be the number of student tickets. There are 20 tickets. Then: $x + y = 20$. The cost of adults' tickets is $8 and for students it is $5, and the total cost is $115. So, $8x + 5y = 115$. Now, we have a system of equations: $\begin{cases} x + y = 20 \\ 8x + 5y = 115 \end{cases}$

Multiply the first equation by -5 and add to the second equation: $-5(x + y = 20) = -5x - 5y = -100$

$8x + 5y + (-5x - 5y) = 115 - 100 \rightarrow 3x = 15 \rightarrow x = 5 \rightarrow 5 + y = 20 \rightarrow y = 15$. There are 5 adult tickets and 15 student tickets.

✍ *Solve each word problem.*

1) A theater is selling tickets for a performance. Mr. Smith purchased 8 senior tickets and 5 child tickets for $136 for his friends and family. Mr. Jackson purchased 4 senior tickets and 6 child tickets for $96. What is the price of a senior ticket? $_____

2) The difference of two numbers is 6. Their sum is 14. What is the bigger number? $_____

3) The sum of the digits of a certain two-digit number is 7. Reversing its digits increase the number by 9. What is the number? _____

4) The difference of two numbers is 18. Their sum is 66. What are the numbers?

_____

Answers – Chapter 13

Systems of Equations

1) $x = 2, y = -\frac{5}{2}$
2) $x = 0, y = -3$
3) $x = 1, y = 2$
4) $x = 20, y = 2$
5) $x = 5, y = 0$
6) $x = 0, y = 2$

Systems of Equations Word Problems

1) $12
2) 10
3) 34
4) 42, 24

Chapter 14: Geometry and Solid Figures

Math Topics that you'll learn Chapter:

- ✓ The Pythagorean Theorem
- ✓ Triangles
- ✓ Polygons
- ✓ Circles
- ✓ Trapezoids
- ✓ Cubes
- ✓ Rectangle Prisms
- ✓ Cylinder

Mathematics is like checkers in being suitable for the young, not too difficult, amusing, and without peril to the state. ~ Plato

The Pythagorean Theorem

Step-by-step guide:

✓ In any right triangle: $a^2 + b^2 = c^2$

Example:

1) Right triangle ABC has two legs of lengths 9 cm (AB) and 12 cm (AC). What is the length of the third side (BC)?

Use Pythagorean Theorem: $a^2 + b^2 = c^2$

Then: $a^2 + b^2 = c^2 \rightarrow 9^2 + 12^2 = c^2 \rightarrow 81 + 144 = c^2$

$c^2 = 225 \rightarrow c = 15\ cm$

2) Find the missing length.

Use Pythagorean Theorem: $a^2 + b^2 = c^2$

Then: $a^2 + b^2 = c^2 \rightarrow 8^2 + 6^2 = c^2 \rightarrow 64 + 36 = c^2$

$c^2 = 100 \rightarrow c = 10$

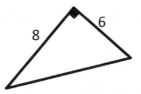

✎ ***Find the missing side?***

1)

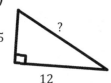

2)

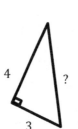

3)

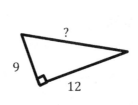

4)

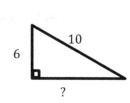

5)

6)

7)

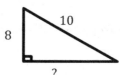

8)

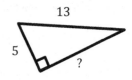

Triangles

Step-by-step guide:

   ✓ In any triangle the sum of all angles is 180 degrees.
   ✓ Area of a triangle = $\frac{1}{2}$ (*base* × *height*)

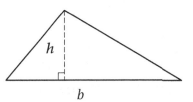

Example:

What is the area of triangles?

1)

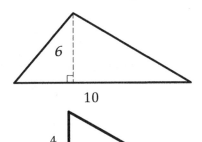

2)

Solution:

Use the are formula: Area = $\frac{1}{2}$ (*base* × *height*)
base = 10 and *height* = 6
Area = $\frac{1}{2}$ (10 × 6) = $\frac{1}{2}$ (60) = 30

Solution:

Use the are formula: Area = $\frac{1}{2}$ (*base* × *height*)
base = 8 and *height* = 4
Area = $\frac{1}{2}$ (8 × 4) = $\frac{32}{2}$ = 16

✍ *Find the measure of the unknown angle in each triangle.*

1)

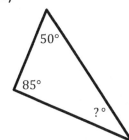

2)

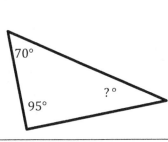

3)

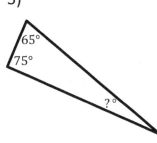

4)

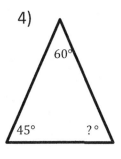

✍ *Find area of each triangle.*

5)

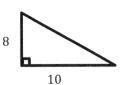

6)

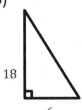

7)

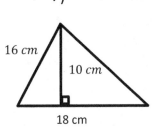

8)

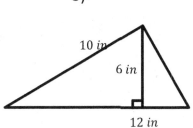

Polygons

Step-by-step guide:

Perimeter of a square $= 4 \times side = 4s$ s	Perimeter of a rectangle $= 2(width + length)$ $width$ $length$
Perimeter of trapezoid $= a + b + c + d$ 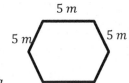	Perimeter of a regular hexagon $= 6a$ 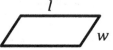 a
Example: Find the perimeter of following regular hexagon. 5 m, 5 m, 5 m, 5 m Perimeter of Pentagon $= 6a$ Perimeter of Pentagon $= 6a = 6 \times 5 = 30\ m$	Perimeter of a parallelogram $= 2(l + w)$ 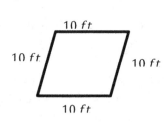 l w

✍ Find the perimeter of each shape.

1)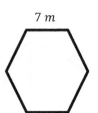
8 cm

2)
14 in
10 in | 10 in
14 in

3)
15 ft 15 ft
15 ft 15 ft

4)
10 ft
10 ft   10 ft
10 ft

5) Regular hexagon
7 m

6)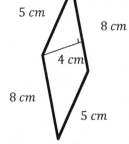
5 cm
8 cm
4 cm
8 cm
5 cm

7) Parallelogram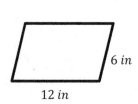
6 in
12 in

8) Square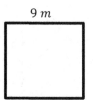
9 m

Circles

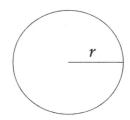

Step-by-step guide:

✓ In a circle, variable r is usually used for the radius and d for diameter and π is about 3.14.

✓ $Area\ of\ a\ circle = \pi r^2$

✓ $Circumference\ of\ a\ circle = 2\pi r$

Example:

1) Find the area of the circle.

Use area formula: $Area = \pi r^2$,

$r = 6\ in$ then: $Area = \pi(6)^2 = 36\pi$, $\pi = 3.14$ then: $Area = 36 \times 3.14 = 113.04\ in^2$

2) Find the Circumference of the circle.

Use Circumference formula: $Circumference = 2\pi r$

$r = 9\ cm$, then: $Circumference = 2\pi(9) = 18\pi$

$\pi = 3.14$ then: $Circumference = 18 \times 3.14 = 56.52\ cm$

✍ **Complete the table below.** ($\pi = 3.14$)

	Radius	Diameter	Circumference	Area
Circle 1	4 *inches*	8 *inches*	25.12 *inches*	50.24 *square inches*
Circle 2		16 *meters*		
Circle 3				50.24 *square ft*
Circle 4			50.24 *miles*	
Circle 5		18 *kilometers*		
Circle 6	7 *centimeters*			
Circle 7		9 *feet*		
Circle 8				19.625 *square meters*

Trapezoids

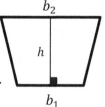

Step-by-step guide:

- ✓ A quadrilateral with at least one pair of parallel sides is a trapezoid.
- ✓ Area of a trapezoid $= \frac{1}{2}h(b_1 + b_2)$

Example:

Calculate the area of the trapezoid.

Use area formula: $A = \frac{1}{2}h(b_1 + b_2)$

$b_1 = 14\ cm$, $b_2 = 18\ cm$ and $h = 20\ cm$

Then: $A = \frac{1}{2}(20)(14 + 18) = 10(32) = 320\ cm^2$

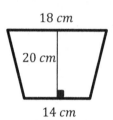

✎ *Find the area of each trapezoid.*

1)

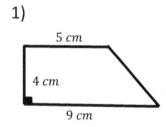

2)

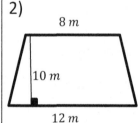

3)

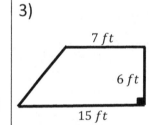

4)

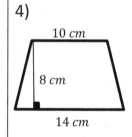

5)

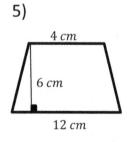

6)

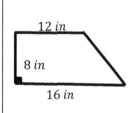

7)

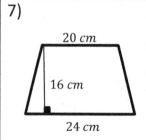

8)

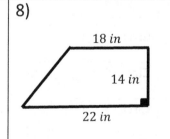

Cubes

Step-by-step guide:

- ✓ A cube is a three-dimensional solid object bounded by six square sides.
- ✓ Volume is the measure of the amount of space inside of a solid figure, like a cube, ball, cylinder or pyramid.
- ✓ Volume of a cube = $(one\ side)^3$
- ✓ surface area of cube = $6 \times (one\ side)^2$

Example:

Find the volume and surface area of this cube.

Use volume formula: $volume = (one\ side)^3$

Then: $volume = (one\ side)^3 = (4)^3 = 64\ cm^3$

Use surface area formula:

$surface\ area\ of\ cube: 6(one\ side)^2 = 6(4)^2 = 6(16) = 96\ cm^2$

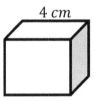
4 cm

✎ *Find the volume of each cube.*

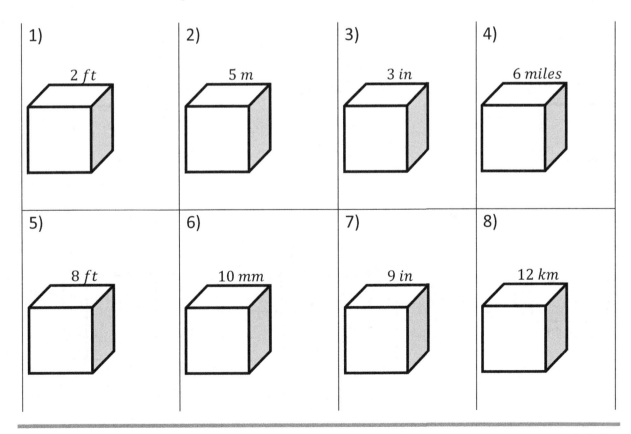

1) 2 ft

2) 5 m

3) 3 in

4) 6 miles

5) 8 ft

6) 10 mm

7) 9 in

8) 12 km

Rectangular Prisms

Step-by-step guide:

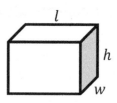

✓ A solid 3-dimensional object which has six rectangular faces.
✓ Volume of a Rectangular prism = **Length × Width × Height**

$Volume = l \times w \times h$ $Surface\ area = 2(wh + lw + lh)$

Example:

Find the volume and surface area of rectangular prism.

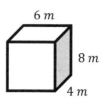

Use volume formula: $Volume = l \times w \times h$

Then: $Volume = 6 \times 4 \times 8 = 192\ m^3$

Use surface area formula: $Surface\ area = 2(wh + lw + lh)$

Then: $Surface\ area = 2\big((4 \times 8) + (6 \times 4) + (6 \times 8)\big)$

$$= 2(32 + 24 + 48) = 2(104) = 208\ m^2$$

✍ *Find the volume of each Rectangular Prism.*

1)

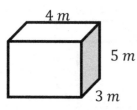

2)

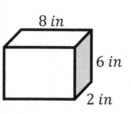

3)

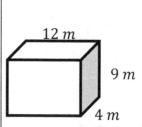

4)

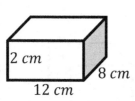

5)

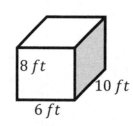

6)

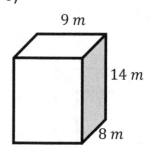

Cylinder

Step-by-step guide:

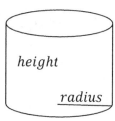

- ✓ A cylinder is a solid geometric figure with straight parallel sides and a circular or oval cross section.
- ✓ Volume of Cylinder Formula $= \pi(radius)^2 \times height$ $\pi = 3.14$
- ✓ Surface area of a cylinder $= 2\pi r^2 + 2\pi rh$

Example:

Find the volume and Surface area of the follow Cylinder.

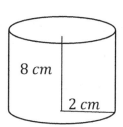

Use volume formula: $Volume = \pi(radius)^2 \times height$
Then: $Volume = \pi(2)^2 \times 8 = \pi 4 \times 8 = 32\pi$
$\pi = 3.14$ then: $Volume = 32\pi = 100.48 \ cm^3$
Use surface area formula: $Surface \ area = 2\pi r^2 + 2\pi rh$
Then: $= 2\pi(2)^2 + 2\pi(2)(8) = 2\pi(4) + 2\pi(16) = 8\pi + 32\pi = 40\pi$
$\pi = 3.14$ then: $Surface \ area = 40 \times 3.14 = 125.6 \ cm^2$

✎ *Find the volume of each Cylinder. Round your answer to the nearest tenth.* ($\pi = 3.14$)

1)

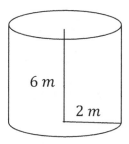

6 m

2 m

2)

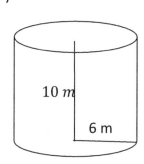

10 m

6 m

3)

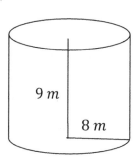

9 m

8 m

4)

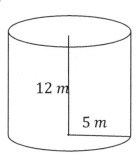

12 m

5 m

5)

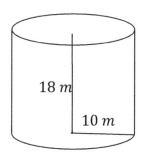

18 m

10 m

6)

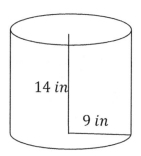

14 in

9 in

Answers – Chapter 14

The Pythagorean Theorem

1) 13
2) 5
3) 15
4) 8

5) 9
6) 20
7) 6
8) 12

Triangles

1) 45°
2) 15°
3) 40°
4) 75°

5) 40 *square unites*
6) 54 *square unites*
7) 90 *square unites*
8) 36 *square unites*

Polygons

1) 32 *cm*
2) 48 *in*
3) 60 *ft*
4) 40 *ft*

5) 42 *m*
6) 26 *cm*
7) 36 *in*
8) 36 *m*

Circles

	Radius	Diameter	Circumference	Area
Circle 1	4 *inches*	8 *inches*	25.12 *inches*	50.24 *square inches*
Circle 2	8 *meters*	16 *meters*	50.24 *meters*	200.96 *square meters*
Circle 3	4 *ft*	8 *ft*	25.12 *ft*	50.24 *square ft*
Circle 4	8 *miles*	16 *miles*	50.24 *miles*	200.96 *square miles*
Circle 5	9 *kilometers*	18 *kilometers*	56.52 *kilometers*	254.34 *sq. kilometers*
Circle 6	7 *centimeters*	14 *centimeters*	43.96 *centimeters*	153.86 *sq. centimeters*
Circle 7	4.5 *feet*	9 *feet*	28.26 *feet*	63.585 *square feet*
Circle 8	2.5 *meters*	5 *meters*	15.7 *meters*	19.625 *square meters*

Trapezoids

1) $28\ cm^2$	5) $48\ cm^2$
2) $100\ m^2$	6) $112\ in^2$
3) $66\ ft^2$	7) $352\ cm^2$
4) $96\ cm^2$	8) $280\ in^2$

Cubes

1) $8\ ft^3$	5) $512\ ft^3$
2) $125\ m^3$	6) $1,000\ mm^3$
3) $27\ in^3$	7) $729\ in^3$
4) $216\ miles^3$	8) $1,728\ km^3$

Rectangle Prisms

1) $60\ m^3$	4) $192\ cm^3$
2) $96\ in^3$	5) $480\ ft^3$
3) $432\ m^3$	6) $1,008\ m^3$

Cylinder

1) $75.36\ m^3$	4) $942\ m^3$
2) $1,130.4\ m^3$	5) $5.652\ m^3$
3) $1,808.64\ m^3$	6) $3,560.76\ in^3$

Chapter 15:
Statistics and Probability

Math Topics that you'll learn Chapter:

- ✓ Mean, Median, Mode, and Range of the Given Data

- ✓ Histograms

- ✓ Pie Graph

- ✓ Probability

Millions saw the apple fall, but Newton asked why." ~ Bernard Baruch

Mean, Median, Mode, and Range of the Given Data

Step-by-step guide:

- ✓ Mean: $\dfrac{\text{sum of the data}}{\text{total number of data entires}}$
- ✓ Mode: value in the list that appears most often
- ✓ Range: the difference of largest value and smallest value in the list

Example:

1) What is the mode of these numbers? $18, 12, 8, 5, 3, 2, 0, 2$

   Mode: value in the list that appears most often
   Therefore: mode is 2

2) What is the median of these numbers? $2, 7, 11, 6, 13, 16, 3$

   Write the numbers in order: $2, 3, 6, 7, 11, 13, 16$

   Median is the number in the middle. Therefore, the median is 7.

✍ *Solve.*

1) Eva went to shop and bought 4 apples, 6 peaches, 3 bananas, 5 pineapple and 8 melons. What are the Mean and Median of her purchase? _____

2) In a javelin throw competition, five athletics score $43, 45, 52, 58$ and 62 meters. What are their Mean and Median? _____

✍ *Find Mode and Rage of the Given Data.*

3) $6, 4, 8, 11, 2, 3$

Mode: _____   Range: _____

4) $5, 7, 3, 12, 7, 10, 6, 9, 4$

Mode: _____   Range: _____

5) $10, 10, 6, 7, 10, 7, 13, 15$

Mode: _____   Range: _____

6) $8, 7, 4, 7, 5, 4, 12, 7$

Mode: _____   Range: _____

Histograms

Step-by-step guide:

✓ A histogram is an accurate representation of the distribution of numerical data.

Example:

Use the following Graph to complete the table.

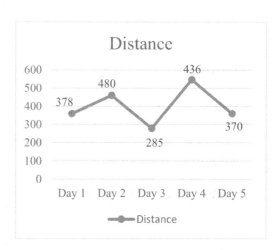

Day	Distance (km)
1	
2	

Answer:

Day	Distance (km)
1	378
2	480
3	285
4	536
5	370

The following table shows the number of births in the US from 2007 to 2012 (in millions).

Year	Number of births (in millions)
2007	4.32
2008	4.25
2009	4.13
2010	4
2011	3.95
2012	3.95

Draw a histogram for the table.

Pie Graph

Step-by-step guide:

✓ A Pie Chart is a circle chart divided into sectors, each sector represents the relative size of each value.

Example:

A library has 670 books that include Mathematics, Physics, Chemistry, English and History. Use following graph to answer question.

What is the number of Mathematics books?

Number of total books $= 670$
Percent of Mathematics books $= 30\% = 0.30$
Then: $0.30 \times 670 = 201$

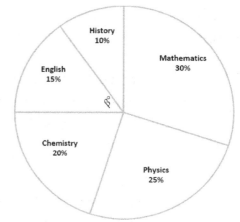

✍ **The circle graph below shows all Jason's expenses for last month. Jason spent $400 on his bills last month.**

1) How much did Jason spend on his car last month? _____

2) How much did Jason spend for foods last month? _____

3) How much did Jason spend on his rent last month? _____

4) What fraction is Jason's expenses for his bills and Car out of his total expenses last month?

Mr. Green's monthly expenses

Probability Problems

Step-by-step guide:

- ✓ Probability is the likelihood of something happening in the future. It is expressed as a number between zero (can never happen) to 1 (will always happen).
- ✓ Probability can be expressed as a fraction, a decimal, or a percent.

Example:

1) If there are 8 red balls and 12 blue balls in a basket, what is the probability that John will pick out a red ball from the basket?

There are 8 red ball and 20 are total number of balls. Therefore, probability that John will pick out a red ball from the basket is 8 out of 20 or $\frac{8}{8+12} = \frac{8}{20} = \frac{2}{5}$.

2) A bag contains 18 balls: two green, five black, eight blue, a brown, a red and one white. If 17 balls are removed from the bag at random, what is the probability that a brown ball has been removed?

If 17 balls are removed from the bag at random, there will be one ball in the bag.

The probability of choosing a brown ball is 1 out of 18. Therefore, the probability of not choosing a brown ball is 17 out of 18 and the probability of having not a brown ball after removing 17 balls is the same.

✎ *Solve.*

1) A number is chosen at random from 1 to 10. Find the probability of selecting number 4 or smaller numbers. _____

2) Bag A contains 9 red marbles and 3 green marbles. Bag B contains 9 black marbles and 6 orange marbles. What is the probability of selecting a green marble at random from bag A? What is the probability of selecting a black marble at random from Bag B? _____ _____

Answers – Chapter 15

Mean, Median, Mode, and Range of the Given Data

1) Mean: 5.2, Median: 5

2) Mean: 52, Median: 52

3) Mode: —, Range: 9

4) Mode: 7, Range: 9

5) Mode: 10, Range: 9

6) Mode: 7, Range: 8

Histograms

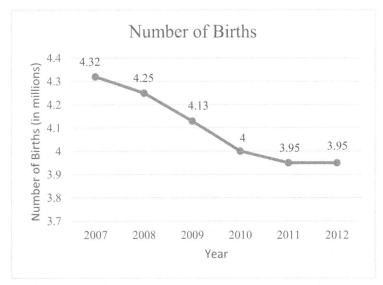

Pie Graph

1) $550
2) $250
3) $675
4) $\frac{19}{50}$

Probability Problems

1) $\frac{2}{5}$

2) $\frac{1}{4}, \frac{3}{5}$

TASC Test Review

The Test Assessing Secondary Completion, commonly known as the TASC or high school equivalency degree, is a standardized test. The TASC is a standardized test to verify that examinees have knowledge in core content areas equivalent to that of graduating high school seniors.

There are five subject area tests on TASC:

- ○ Reading;
- ○ Writing;
- ○ Social Studies;
- ○ Science;
- ○ Mathematics.

The TASC Mathematics test is a 105-minute test that covers basic mathematics topics, quantitative problem-solving and algebraic questions. There are two Mathematics sections on the TASC. The first section contains 40 multiple choice questions where calculators are permitted. You have 55 minutes to complete this section. The second section contains 12 Gridded-Response questions. Calculator is NOT allowed in the second part. Test takers have 50 minutes to answer all questions in this section. Examinees will also be given a page of mathematic formulas to use during the test.

In this section, there are two complete TASC Mathematics Tests. Take these tests to see what score you'll be able to receive on a real TASC test.

Good luck!

Time to refine your quantitative reasoning skill with a practice test

Take these tests to simulate the test day experience. After you've finished, score your tests using the answer keys.

Before You Start

- You'll need a pencil, a calculator, and a timer to take the test.

- It's okay to guess. You won't lose any points if you're wrong. So be sure to answer every question.

- After you've finished the test, review the answer key to see where you went wrong.

- **Calculators are only permitted for the first section of the TASC Test.**

- The TASC Mathematics test contains a formula sheet, which displays formulas relating to geometric measurement and certain algebra concepts. Formulas are provided to test-takers so that they may focus on application, rather than the memorization, of formulas.

- For each multiple-choice question, there are four possible answers. Choose which one is best. For grids in questions, write your answer in the answer boxes at the top of the grid. Then, as shown below fill in a bubble under each box in which you wrote your answer.

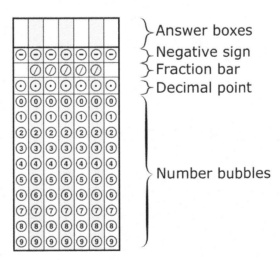

Good Luck!

TASC Mathematics
Practice Test 1

2019

Two Parts

Total number of questions: 52

Part 1 (Calculator): 40 questions

Part 2 (Calculator): 12 questions

Total time for two parts: 105 Minutes

TASC Practice Tests Answer Sheet

Remove (or photocopy) these answer sheets and use them to complete the practice tests.

TASC Practice Test 1 – Section 1 Answer Sheet

1 Ⓐ Ⓑ Ⓒ Ⓓ	9 Ⓐ Ⓑ Ⓒ Ⓓ	17 Ⓐ Ⓑ Ⓒ Ⓓ	25 Ⓐ Ⓑ Ⓒ Ⓓ	33 Ⓐ Ⓑ Ⓒ Ⓓ
2 Ⓐ Ⓑ Ⓒ Ⓓ	10 Ⓐ Ⓑ Ⓒ Ⓓ	18 Ⓐ Ⓑ Ⓒ Ⓓ	26 Ⓐ Ⓑ Ⓒ Ⓓ	34 Ⓐ Ⓑ Ⓒ Ⓓ
3 Ⓐ Ⓑ Ⓒ Ⓓ	11 Ⓐ Ⓑ Ⓒ Ⓓ	19 Ⓐ Ⓑ Ⓒ Ⓓ	27 Ⓐ Ⓑ Ⓒ Ⓓ	35 Ⓐ Ⓑ Ⓒ Ⓓ
4 Ⓐ Ⓑ Ⓒ Ⓓ	12 Ⓐ Ⓑ Ⓒ Ⓓ	20 Ⓐ Ⓑ Ⓒ Ⓓ	28 Ⓐ Ⓑ Ⓒ Ⓓ	36 Ⓐ Ⓑ Ⓒ Ⓓ
5 Ⓐ Ⓑ Ⓒ Ⓓ	13 Ⓐ Ⓑ Ⓒ Ⓓ	21 Ⓐ Ⓑ Ⓒ Ⓓ	29 Ⓐ Ⓑ Ⓒ Ⓓ	37 Ⓐ Ⓑ Ⓒ Ⓓ
6 Ⓐ Ⓑ Ⓒ Ⓓ	14 Ⓐ Ⓑ Ⓒ Ⓓ	22 Ⓐ Ⓑ Ⓒ Ⓓ	30 Ⓐ Ⓑ Ⓒ Ⓓ	38 Ⓐ Ⓑ Ⓒ Ⓓ
7 Ⓐ Ⓑ Ⓒ Ⓓ	15 Ⓐ Ⓑ Ⓒ Ⓓ	23 Ⓐ Ⓑ Ⓒ Ⓓ	31 Ⓐ Ⓑ Ⓒ Ⓓ	39 Ⓐ Ⓑ Ⓒ Ⓓ
8 Ⓐ Ⓑ Ⓒ Ⓓ	16 Ⓐ Ⓑ Ⓒ Ⓓ	24 Ⓐ Ⓑ Ⓒ Ⓓ	32 Ⓐ Ⓑ Ⓒ Ⓓ	40 Ⓐ Ⓑ Ⓒ Ⓓ

TASC Practice Test 1: Section 2: Grid-ins Questions

41   42   43   44

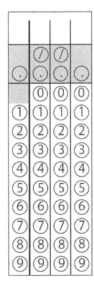

45

46

47

48

49

50

51

52

TASC Mathematics

Practice Test 1

Part 1 (Calculator)

Total number of questions: 40

Total time for Part 1 (Calculator): 55 Minutes

You may use a calculator on this part.

Mathematics Reference Sheet

Cylinder: $v = \pi r^2 h$

Pyramid: $v = \frac{1}{3} bh$

cone: $v = \frac{1}{3} \pi r^2 h$

Sphere: $\frac{4}{3} \pi r^3$

coordinate Geometry

Midpoint of the segment AB:

$M\left(\dfrac{x_1 + x_2}{2}, \dfrac{y_1 + y_2}{2}\right)$

Distance from A to B:

$d = \sqrt{(x_1 - x_2)^2 + (y_1 - y_2)^2}$

Slope of a line:

$m = \dfrac{y_2 - y_1}{x_2 - x_1} = \dfrac{rise}{run}$

Special Factoring

$a^2 - b^2 = (a + b)(a - b)$

$a^2 + 2ab + b^2 = (a + b)(a + b)$

$a^2 - 2ab + b^2 = (a - b)(a - b)$

$a^3 + b^3 = (a + b)(a^2 - ab + b^2)$

$a^3 - b^3 = (a - b)(a^2 + ab + b^2)$

Quadratic Formula

for $ax^2 + bx + c = 0$

$x = \dfrac{-b \pm \sqrt{b^2 - 4ac}}{2a}$

Interest

Simple Interest:

$I = prt$

Interest Formula (compounded n times per year):

$A = p\left(1 + \dfrac{r}{n}\right)^{nt}$

A = Amount after t years.

p = principal

r = annual interest rate

t = time in years

I = Interest

Trigonometric Identities

Pythagorean Theorem: $a^2 + b^2 = c^2$

$\sin \theta = \dfrac{opp}{hyp}$

$\cos \theta = \dfrac{adj}{hyp}$

$\tan \theta = \dfrac{opp}{adj}$

$sin^2\theta + cos^2\theta = 1$

$Density = \dfrac{Mass}{Volume}$

Central Angle	Inscribed Angle	Intersecting Chords Theorem
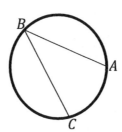	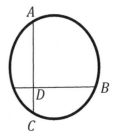	
$m\angle AOB = m\widehat{AB}$	$m\angle ABC = \frac{1}{2}m\,\widehat{AC}$	$A \cdot B = C \cdot D$

Probability

Permutations: $_nP_r = \dfrac{n!}{(n-r)!}$

Combinations: $_nC_r = \dfrac{n!}{(n-r)!r!}$

Multiplication rule (independent events): P(A and B) = P(A)·P(B)

Multiplication rule (general): P(A and B) = P(A)·P(B|A)

Addition rule: P(A or B) = P(A) + P(B) − P(A and B)

Conditional Probability: P(B|A) = $\dfrac{P(A\ and\ B)}{P(A)}$

Arithmetic Sequence: $a_n = a_1 + (n-1)d$ where a_n is the nth term, a_1 is the first term, and d is the common difference.

Geometric Sequence: $a_n = a_1 r^{(n-1)}$ where a_n is the nth term, a_1 is the first term, and r is the common ratio.

1) In the figure below, what is the value of x?

A. 43

B. 67

C. 77

D. 90

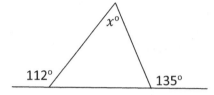

2) Simplify the expression.

$$(8x^3 - 8x^2 + 2x^4) - (4x^2 - 2x^4 + 2x^3)$$

A. $4x^4 + 6x^3 - 12x^2$

B. $4x^3 - 12x^2$

C. $4x^4 + 4x^3 - 12x^2$

D. $8x^3 - 12x^2$

3) In two successive years, the population of a town is increased by 15% and 20%. What percent of the population is increased after two years?

A. 32%

B. 35%

C. 38%

D. 68%

4) Which of the following answers represents the compound inequality $-2 \leq 2x - 4 < 8$?

A. $2 < x < 4$

B. $2 \leq x \leq 4$

C. $1 < x \leq 6$

D. $1 \leq x < 6$

5) What is the volume of a box with the following dimensions?

Hight = 4 cm Width = 5 cm Length = 6 cm

A. 15 cm^3

B. 60 cm^3

C. 90 cm^3

D. 120 cm^3

6) Mr. Carlos family are choosing a menu for their reception. They have 6 choices of appetizers, 5 choices of entrees, 4 choices of cake. How many different menu combinations are possible for them to choose?

A. 12

B. 32

C. 120

D. 150

7) In a stadium the ratio of home fans to visiting fans in a crowd is 5: 7. Which of the following could be the total number of fans in the stadium?

A. 12,324

B. 42,326

C. 44,566

D. 66,812

8) Last week 24,000 fans attended a football match. This week three times as many bought tickets, but one sixth of them cancelled their tickets. How many are attending this week?

A. 48,000

B. 54,000

C. 60,000

D. 72,000

9) What is the perimeter of a square in centimeters that has an area of 595.36 cm^2 ?

A. 97.6

B. 96.2

C. 95.7

D. 92.6

10) Which of the following points lies on the line $x + 2y = 4$?

A. $(-4, 4)$

B. $(1, 2)$

C. $(-1, 3)$

D. $(-3, 4)$

11) The perimeter of a rectangular yard is 60 meters. What is its length if its width is twice its length?

A. 10 $meters$

B. 18 $meters$

C. 20 $meters$

D. 24 $meters$

12) Which of the following shows the numbers in descending order?

$$\frac{1}{3}, \ 0.68 \ , 67\% \ , \frac{4}{5}$$

A. $67\%, 0.68, \frac{1}{3}, \frac{4}{5}$

B. $67\%, 0.68, \frac{4}{5}, \frac{1}{3}$

C. $0.68, 67\%, \frac{1}{3} \ , \frac{4}{5}$

D. $\frac{1}{3}, 67\%, 0.68, \frac{4}{5}$

13) The mean of 50 test scores was calculated as 90. But, it turned out that one of the scores was misread as 94 but it was 69. What is the correct mean of the test scores?

A. 85

B. 87

C. 89.5

D. 90.5

14) Two dice are thrown simultaneously, what is the probability of getting a sum of 5 or 8?

A. $\frac{1}{3}$

B. $\frac{11}{36}$

C. $\frac{1}{2}$

D. $\frac{1}{4}$

15) A swimming pool holds 2,000 cubic feet of water. The swimming pool is 25 feet long and 10 feet wide. How deep is the swimming pool?

A. 2
B. 4
C. 6
D. 8

16) What is the area of a square whose diagonal is 8?

A. 16

B. 32

C. 36

D. 64

17) Anita's trick–or–treat bag contains 12 pieces of chocolate, 18 suckers, 18 pieces of gum, 24 pieces of licorice. If she randomly pulls a piece of candy from her bag, what is the probability of her pulling out a piece of sucker?

A. $\dfrac{1}{3}$

B. $\dfrac{1}{4}$

C. $\dfrac{1}{6}$

D. $\dfrac{1}{12}$

18) The average of 6 numbers is 12. The average of 4 of those numbers is 10. What is the average of the other two numbers?

A. 10

B. 12

C. 14

D. 16

19) What is the value of x in the following system of equations?

$$2x + 5y = 11$$
$$4x - 2y = -26$$

A. -4

B. $\dfrac{9}{2}$

C. $-\dfrac{9}{2}$

D. 4

20) The perimeter of the trapezoid below is 36 cm. What is its area?

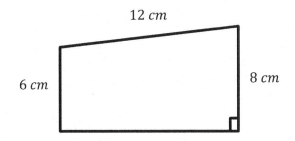

A. 576 cm^2

B. 70 cm^2

C. 48 cm^2

D. 24 cm^2

21) If 150% of a number is 75, then what is the 80% of that number?

A. 40

B. 50

C. 70

D. 85

22) A football team had $20,000 to spend on supplies. The team spent $14,000 on new balls. New sport shoes cost $160 each. Which of the following inequalities represent the number of new shoes the team can purchase.

A. $160x + 14,000 \leq 20,000$

B. $160x + 14,000 \geq 20,000$

C. $14,000x + 160 \leq 20,000$

D. $14,000x + 160x \geq 20,000$

23) A card is drawn at random from a standard 52–card deck, what is the probability that the card is of Hearts? (The deck includes 13 of each suit clubs, diamonds, hearts, and spades)

A. $\dfrac{1}{3}$

B. $\dfrac{1}{4}$

C. $\dfrac{1}{6}$

D. $\dfrac{1}{52}$

24) The average of five numbers is 26. If a sixth number that is greater than 42 is added, then, which of the following could be the new average?

A. 25

B. 26

C. 28.66

D. 29

25) The diagonal of a rectangle is 13 inches long and the height of the rectangle is 5 inches. What is the area of the rectangle in inches?

A. $42\ in^2$

B. $50\ in^2$

C. $60\ in^2$

D. $65\ in^2$

26) The ratio of boys and girls in a class is $4:7$. If there are 66 students in the class, how many more boys should be enrolled to make the ratio $1:1$?

A. 8

B. 10

C. 18

D. 20

27) Mr. Jones saves $2,500 out of his monthly family income of $55,000. What fractional part of his income does he save?

A. $\frac{1}{22}$

B. $\frac{1}{11}$

C. $\frac{3}{25}$

D. $\frac{2}{15}$

28) Jason needs an 77% average in his writing class to pass. On his first 4 exams, he earned scores of 68%, 72%, 85%, and 90%. What is the minimum score Jason can earn on his fifth and final test to pass?

A.   375%

B.   315%

C.   90%

D.   70%

29) What is the value of x in the following equation?

$$\frac{2}{3}x + \frac{1}{6} = \frac{1}{2}$$

A. 6

B. $\frac{1}{3}$

C. $\frac{1}{2}$

D. $\frac{1}{4}$

30) What is the surface area of the cylinder below?

A. $40\ \pi\ in^2$

B. $57\ \pi\ in^2$

C. $66\ \pi\ in^2$

D. $288\ \pi\ in^2$

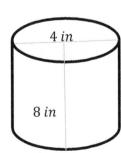

31) The square of a number is $\frac{25}{64}$. What is the cube of that number?

A. $\frac{5}{8}$

B. $\frac{25}{254}$

C. $\frac{125}{512}$

D. $\frac{125}{64}$

32) What is the median of these numbers? $2, 27, 28, 19, 67, 44, 35$

A. 19

B. 28

C. 44

D. 35

33) Right triangle ABC has two legs of lengths $6\ cm$ (AB) and $8\ cm$ (AC). What is the length of the third side (BC)?

A. $4\ cm$
B. $6\ cm$
C. $8\ cm$
D. $10\ cm$

34) What is the equivalent temperature of $104°F$ in Celsius?

$$C = \frac{5}{9}(F - 32)$$

A. 32

B. 40

C. 48

D. 52

35) If 40% of a number is 4, what is the number?

A. 4

B. 8

C. 10

D. 12

36) The circle graph below shows all Mr. Green's expenses for last month. If he spent $560 on his car, how much did he spend for his rent?

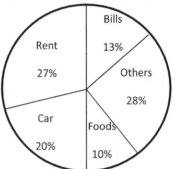

Mr. Green's monthly expenses

A. $600

B. $640

C. $680

D. $756

37) Jason is 15 miles ahead of Joe running at 5.5 miles per hour and Joe is running at the speed of 7 miles per hour. How long does it take Joe to catch Jason?

A. 3 *hours*

B. 4 *hours*

C. 10 *hours*

D. 15 *hours*

38) 44 students took an exam and 11 of them failed. What percent of the students passed the exam?

A. 20%

B. 40%

C. 60%

D. 75%

39) A bank is offering 3.5% simple interest on a savings account. If you deposit $12,000, how much interest will you earn in two years?

A. $420

B. $840

C. $4200

D. $8400

40) Simplify $6x^2y^3(2x^2y)^3 =$

A. $12x^4y^6$

B. $12x^8y^6$

C. $48x^4y^6$

D. $48x^8y^6$

IF YOU FINISH BEFORE TIME IS CALLED, YOU MAY CHECK YOUR WORK ON THIS SECTION ONLY. DO NOT TURN TO OTHER SECTION IN THE TEST. STOP

TASC Mathematics

Practice Test 1

Part 2 (Non-Calculator)

Total number of questions: 12

Total time for Part 1 (Calculator): 50 Minutes

You may NOT use a calculator on this part.

41) $[-3 \times (-14) - 48] - (-14) + [3 \times 8] \div 2 = ?$

42) A tree 32 feet tall casts a shadow 12 feet long. Jack is 6 feet tall. How long is Jack's shadow?

43) What is the product of all possible values of x in the following equation?

$$|2x - 6| = 12$$

44) What is the slope of a line that is perpendicular to the line $3x + y = 6$?

45) What is the value of the expression $3(x - 2y) + (2 - x)^2$ when $x = 5$ and $= -3$?

46) What is the value of x in the following equation? $-60 = 115 - x$

47) The area of a rectangular yard is 90 square meters. What is its width if its length is 15 meters?

48) If $4x - 1 = 9$, what is the value of $2x + 10$?

49) The average weight of 18 girls in a class is 60 kg and the average weight of 32 boys in the same class is 66 kg. What is the average weight of all the 50 students in that class? (round your answer to the nearest hundredth)

50) The width of a box is one third of its length. The height of the box is one third of its width. If the length of the box is $27 \ cm$, what is the volume of the box?

51) In a classroom of 60 students, 42 are female. What percentage of the class is male?

52) Two third of 21 is equal to $\frac{2}{5}$ of what number?

IF YOU FINISH BEFORE TIME IS CALLED, YOU MAY CHECK YOUR WORK ON THIS SECTION ONLY. DO NOT TURN TO OTHER SECTION IN THE TEST.

STOP

TASC Mathematics
Practice Test 2

2019

Two Parts

Total number of questions: 52

Part 1 (Calculator): 40 questions

Part 2 (Calculator): 12 questions

Total time for two parts: 105 Minutes

TASC Practice Tests Answer Sheet

Remove (or photocopy) these answer sheets and use them to complete the practice tests.

TASC Practice Test 2 – Section 1 Answer Sheet

1 Ⓐ Ⓑ Ⓒ Ⓓ	9 Ⓐ Ⓑ Ⓒ Ⓓ	17 Ⓐ Ⓑ Ⓒ Ⓓ	25 Ⓐ Ⓑ Ⓒ Ⓓ	33 Ⓐ Ⓑ Ⓒ Ⓓ
2 Ⓐ Ⓑ Ⓒ Ⓓ	10 Ⓐ Ⓑ Ⓒ Ⓓ	18 Ⓐ Ⓑ Ⓒ Ⓓ	26 Ⓐ Ⓑ Ⓒ Ⓓ	34 Ⓐ Ⓑ Ⓒ Ⓓ
3 Ⓐ Ⓑ Ⓒ Ⓓ	11 Ⓐ Ⓑ Ⓒ Ⓓ	19 Ⓐ Ⓑ Ⓒ Ⓓ	27 Ⓐ Ⓑ Ⓒ Ⓓ	35 Ⓐ Ⓑ Ⓒ Ⓓ
4 Ⓐ Ⓑ Ⓒ Ⓓ	12 Ⓐ Ⓑ Ⓒ Ⓓ	20 Ⓐ Ⓑ Ⓒ Ⓓ	28 Ⓐ Ⓑ Ⓒ Ⓓ	36 Ⓐ Ⓑ Ⓒ Ⓓ
5 Ⓐ Ⓑ Ⓒ Ⓓ	13 Ⓐ Ⓑ Ⓒ Ⓓ	21 Ⓐ Ⓑ Ⓒ Ⓓ	29 Ⓐ Ⓑ Ⓒ Ⓓ	37 Ⓐ Ⓑ Ⓒ Ⓓ
6 Ⓐ Ⓑ Ⓒ Ⓓ	14 Ⓐ Ⓑ Ⓒ Ⓓ	22 Ⓐ Ⓑ Ⓒ Ⓓ	30 Ⓐ Ⓑ Ⓒ Ⓓ	38 Ⓐ Ⓑ Ⓒ Ⓓ
7 Ⓐ Ⓑ Ⓒ Ⓓ	15 Ⓐ Ⓑ Ⓒ Ⓓ	23 Ⓐ Ⓑ Ⓒ Ⓓ	31 Ⓐ Ⓑ Ⓒ Ⓓ	39 Ⓐ Ⓑ Ⓒ Ⓓ
8 Ⓐ Ⓑ Ⓒ Ⓓ	16 Ⓐ Ⓑ Ⓒ Ⓓ	24 Ⓐ Ⓑ Ⓒ Ⓓ	32 Ⓐ Ⓑ Ⓒ Ⓓ	40 Ⓐ Ⓑ Ⓒ Ⓓ

TASC Practice Test 2: Section 2: Grid-ins Questions

41 42 43 44

45

46

47

48

49

50

51

52

TASC Mathematics

Practice Test 2

Part 1 (Calculator)

Total number of questions: 40

Total time for Part 1 (Calculator): 55 Minutes

You may use a calculator on this part.

Mathematics Reference Sheet

Cylinder: $v = \pi r^2 h$

Pyramid: $v = \frac{1}{3} bh$

cone: $v = \frac{1}{3} \pi r^2 h$

Sphere: $\frac{4}{3} \pi r^3$

coordinate Geometry

Midpoint of the segment AB:

$$M \left(\frac{x_1 + x_2}{2}, \frac{y_1 + y_2}{2} \right)$$

Distance from A to B:

$$d = \sqrt{(x_1 - x_2)^2 + (y_1 - y_2)^2}$$

Slope of a line:

$$m = \frac{y_2 - y_1}{x_2 - x_1} = \frac{rise}{run}$$

Special Factoring

$a^2 - b^2 = (a + b)(a - b)$

$a^2 + 2ab + b^2 = (a + b)(a + b)$

$a^2 - 2ab + b^2 = (a - b)(a - b)$

$a^3 + b^3 = (a + b)(a^2 - ab + b^2)$

$a^3 - b^3 = (a - b)(a^2 + ab + b^2)$

Quadratic Formula

for $ax^2 + bx + c = 0$

$$x = \frac{-b \pm \sqrt{b^2 - 4ac}}{2a}$$

Interest

Simple Interest:

$$I = prt$$

Interest Formula (compounded n times per year):

$$A = p\left(1 + \frac{r}{n}\right)^{nt}$$

A = Amount after t years.

p = principal

r = annual interest rate

t = time in years

I = Interest

Trigonometric Identities

Pythagorean Theorem: $a^2 + b^2 = c^2$

$\sin \theta = \frac{opp}{hyp}$

$\cos \theta = \frac{adj}{hyp}$

$\tan \theta = \frac{opp}{adj}$

$\sin^2 \theta + \cos^2 \theta = 1$

$\text{Density} = \frac{Mass}{Volume}$

Central Angle	Inscribed Angle	Intersecting Chords Theorem
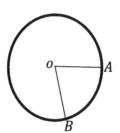	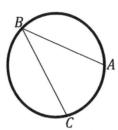	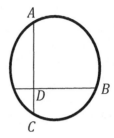
$m\angle AOB = m\widehat{AB}$	$m\angle ABC = \frac{1}{2}m\widehat{AC}$	$A \cdot B = C \cdot D$

Probability

Permutations: $_nP_r = \dfrac{n!}{(n-r)!}$

Combinations: $_nC_r = \dfrac{n!}{(n-r)!r!}$

Multiplication rule (independent events): P(A and B) = P(A)·P(B)

Multiplication rule (general): P(A and B) = P(A)·P(B|A)

Addition rule: P(A or B) = P(A) + P(B) − P(A and B)

Conditional Probability: $P(B|A) = \dfrac{P(A \ and \ B)}{P(A)}$

Arithmetic Sequence: $a_n = a_1 + (n-1)d$ where a_n is the nth term, a_1 is the first term, and d is the common difference.

Geometric Sequence: $a_n = a_1 r^{(n-1)}$ where a_n is the nth term, a_1 is the first term, and r is the common ratio.

1) If 90% of A is 30% of B, then B is what percent of A?

A. 3%
B. 30%
C. 200%
D. 300%

2) How many possible outfit combinations come from five shirts, four slacks, and seven ties?

A. 16
B. 20
C. 70
D. 140

3) A bank is offering 8.5% simple interest on a savings account. If you deposit $12,000, how much interest will you earn in five years?

A. $1,300
B. $2,600
C. $5,100
D. $7,200

4) Which of the following could be the product of two consecutive prime numbers?

A. 2
B. 6
C. 14
D. 19

5) Which of the following lists shows the fractions in order from least to greatest?
$$\frac{3}{4}, \frac{2}{7}, \frac{3}{8}, \frac{7}{11}$$

A. $\frac{3}{8}, \frac{2}{7}, \frac{3}{4}, \frac{7}{11}$

B. $\frac{2}{7}, \frac{7}{11}, \frac{3}{8}, \frac{3}{4}$

C. $\frac{2}{7}, \frac{3}{8}, \frac{7}{11}, \frac{3}{4}$

D. $\frac{3}{8}, \frac{2}{7}, \frac{7}{11}, \frac{3}{4}$

6) What is the value of 5^5?

A. 25
B. 125
C. 625
D. 3,125

7) 15 is What percent of 25?

A. 30%
B. 55%
C. 60%
D. 80%

8) Two third of 18 is equal to $\frac{2}{5}$ of what number?

A. 12
B. 20
C. 30
D. 60

9) The price of a car was $28,000 in 2012. In 2013, the price of that car was $18,200. What was the rate of depreciation of the price of car per year?

A. 20%
B. 30%
C. 35%
D. 40%

10) The width of a box is one third of its length. The height of the box is half of its width. If the length of the box is 24 cm, what is the volume of the box?

A. $72\ cm^3$
B. $144\ cm^3$
C. $288\ cm^3$
D. $768\ cm^3$

11) The marked price of a computer is D dollar. Its price decreased by 25% in January and later increased by 20% in February. What is the final price of the computer in D dollar?

A. 0.80 D
B. 0.90 D
C. 0.95 D
D. 1.20 D

12) A $50 shirt now selling for $38 is discounted by what percent?

A. 14%
B. 24%
C. 34%
D. 68%

13) A boat sails 90 miles south and then 120 miles east. How far is the boat from its start point?

A. 140 $miles$
B. 150 $miles$
C. 160 $miles$
D. 170 $miles$

14) The ratio of boys and girls in a class is 4: 7. If there are 77 students in the class, how many more boys should be enrolled to make the ratio 1: 1?

A. 8
B. 15
C. 21
D. 30

15) Sophia purchased a sofa for $250.50 . The sofa is regularly priced at $300. What was the percent discount Sophia received on the sofa?

A. 14.50%
B. 16.50%
C. 18%
D. 18.50%

16) The score of Emma was half as that of Ava and the score of Mia was twice that of Ava. If the score of Mia was 80, what is the score of Emma?

A. 12
B. 15
C. 20
D. 30

17) A bag contains 20 balls: four green, five black, eight blue, a brown, a red and one white. If 19 balls are removed from the bag at random, what is the probability that a brown ball has been removed?

A. $\dfrac{1}{9}$

B. $\dfrac{1}{6}$

C. $\dfrac{16}{17}$

D. $\dfrac{19}{20}$

18) How many tiles of $8\ cm^2$ is needed to cover a floor of dimension $8\ cm$ by $32\ cm$?

A. 8
B. 18
C. 32
D. 56

19) A rope weighs 800 grams per meter of length. What is the weight in kilograms of 14.4 meters of this rope? ($1\ kilograms = 1,000\ grams$)

A. 1.152 kg
B. 11.52 kg
C. 115.2 kg
D. 1152 kg

20) When a number is subtracted from 18 and the difference is divided by that number, the result is 5. What is the value of the number?

A. 1
B. 2
C. 3
D. 6

21) An angle is equal to one fourth of its supplement. What is the measure of that angle?

A. 36
B. 25
C. 15
D. 10

22) John traveled $160 \ km$ in $4 \ hours$ and Alice traveled $210 \ km$ in $3 \ hours$. What is the ratio of the average speed of John to average speed of Alice?

A. 4: 3
B. 3: 5
C. 4: 7
D. 7: 9

23) The diagonal of a rectangle is 10 inches long and the height of the rectangle is 8 inches. What is the perimeter of the rectangle in inches?

A. 28
B. 26
C. 22
D. 18

24) The average of five consecutive numbers is 38. What is the smallest number?

A. 38
B. 36
C. 34
D. 12

25) Find the average of the following numbers: $12, 10, 4, 8, 11, 9$

A. 5
B. 9.5
C. 9
D. 11

26) The average weight of 20 girls in a class is $58\ kg$ and the average weight of 30 boys in the same class is $66\ kg$. What is the average weight of all the 50 students in that class?

A. 62
B. 62.8
C. 62.08
D. 62.88

27) The price of a laptop is decreased by 20% to $420. What is its original price?

A. $480
B. $500
C. $525
D. $550

28) What is the median of these numbers? $5, 10, 14, 9, 19, 6\ 16$

A. 9
B. 10
C. 14
D. 16

29) A taxi driver earns $9 per 1-hour work. If he works 10 hours a day and in 1 hour he uses 2-liters petrol with price $1 for 1-liter. How much money does he earn in one day?

A. $90
B. $88
C. $70
D. $60
30)

31) The radius of a cylinder is 8 inches and its height is 16 inches. What is the surface area of the cylinder in square inches? ($\pi = 3.14$)

A.   423.4

B.   876.12

C.   928.28

D.   1,205.76

32) How long does a 390–miles trip take moving at 60 miles per hour (mph)?

A.   6 $hours$

B.   6 $hours$ and 50 $minutes$

C.   6 $hours$ and 30 $minutes$

D.   8 $hours$ and 35 $minutes$

32) In the xy-plane, the point $(1, 2)$ and $(-1, 6)$ are on line A. Which of the following points could also be on line A? (Select one or more answer choices)

A. $(-1, 2)$

B. $(5, 7)$

C. $(3, 4)$

D. $(3, -2)$

33) In 1999, the average worker's income increased $2,000 per year starting from $23,000 annual salary. Which equation represents income greater than average? (I = income, x = number of years after 1999)

A. $I > 2000x + 23000$

B. $I > -2000x + 23000$

C. $I < -2000x + 23000$

D. $I < 2000x - 23000$

34) The price of a sofa is decreased by 18% to $451. What was its original price?

A. $480
B. $535
C. $550
D. $680

35) Right triangle ABC has two legs of lengths $3\ cm$ (AB) and $4\ cm$ (AC). What is the length of the third side (BC)?

A. $15\ cm$
B. $14\ cm$
C. $8\ cm$
D. $5\ cm$

36) If 50% of a class are girls, and 30% of girls play tennis, what percent of the class play tennis?

A. 10%
B. 15%
C. 20%
D. 40%

37) In five successive hours, a car traveled $40\ km$, $45\ km$, $50\ km$, $35\ km$ and $55\ km$. In the next five hours, it traveled with an average speed of $75\ km\ per\ hour$. Find the total distance the car traveled in $10\ hours$.

A. $425\ km$
B. $550\ km$
C. $600\ km$
D. $670\ km$

38) The area of a circle is less than 64π. Which of the following can be the circumference of the circle?
A. 12π
B. 16π
C. 24π
D. 32π

39) Which of the following values for x and y satisfy the following system of equations?

$$\begin{cases} x + 4y = 10 \\ 5x + 5y = 20 \end{cases}$$

A. $x = -2, y = -2$
B. $x = 2, y - 3$
C. $x = 2, y = 2$
D. $x = 3, y = -2$

40) A chemical solution contains 6% alcohol. If there is $42\ ml$ of alcohol, what is the volume of the solution?

A. $140\ ml$
B. $380\ ml$
C. $700\ ml$
D. $1,100\ ml$

IF YOU FINISH BEFORE TIME IS CALLED, YOU MAY CHECK YOUR WORK ON THIS SECTION ONLY. DO NOT TURN TO OTHER SECTION IN THE TEST.

STOP

TASC Mathematics

Practice Test 2

Part 2 (Non-Calculator)

Total number of questions: 12

Total time for Part 1 (Calculator): 50 Minutes

You may NOT use a calculator on this part.

41) $32 - 3 \times (6) - [8 + 16 \times (-5)] \div 2 - 12 = ?$

42) What is the area of an isosceles right triangle that has one leg that measures 8?

43) The average of $11, 13, 18$ and x is 20. What is the value of x?

44) The perimeter of the trapezoid below is 62. What is its area?

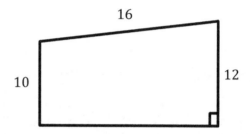

45) From last year, the price of gasoline has increased from $2.50 per gallon to $2.75 per gallon. The new price is what percent of the original price?

46) If $2x - 6 = 6.5$, What is the value of $-3x + 20$?

47) If 75% of a class are girls, and $\frac{1}{3}$ of girls take drawing class this semester, what percent of the class are girls who take drawing class this semester?

48) If $\frac{x-4}{6} = N$ and $N = 8$, what is the value of x?

49) Jason purchased a laptop for $529.72. The laptop is regularly priced at $646.00. What was the percent discount Jason received on the laptop?

50) What is the value of $f(-2)$ for the following function f?
$$f(x) = 2x^2 + 4x$$

51) If the ratio of $5a$ to $2b$ is $\frac{1}{6}$, what is the ratio of a to b?

52) A construction company is building a wall. The company can build $40\ cm$ of the wall per minute. After 50 minutes $\frac{2}{3}$ of the wall is completed. How many meters is the wall?

IF YOU FINISH BEFORE TIME IS CALLED, YOU MAY CHECK YOUR WORK ON THIS SECTION ONLY. DO NOT TURN TO OTHER SECTION IN THE TEST. STOP

TASC Mathematics Practice Tests Answer Keys

Now, it's time to review your results to see where you went wrong and what areas you need to improve.

								TASC Practice Test 1													TASC Practice Test 2			
1	B	16	B	31	C	41	**20**	1	D	16	C	31	C	41	**38**
2	A	17	B	32	B	42	**2.25**	2	D	17	D	32	D	42	**32**
3	C	18	D	33	D	43	**−27**	3	C	18	C	33	A	43	**38**
4	D	19	C	34	B	44	**1/3**	4	B	19	B	34	C	44	**264**
5	D	20	B	35	C	45	**42**	5	C	20	C	35	D	45	**110**
6	C	21	A	36	D	46	**175**	6	D	21	A	36	B	46	**1.25**
7	A	22	A	37	C	47	**6**	7	C	22	C	37	C	47	**25**
8	C	23	B	38	D	48	**15**	8	C	23	A	38	A	48	**52**
9	A	24	D	39	B	49	**63.84**	9	C	24	B	39	C	49	**18**
10	A	25	C	40	D	50	**729**	10	D	25	C	40	C	50	**0**
11	A	26	C			51	**30**	11	B	26	B			51	**0.06**
12	D	27	A			52	**35**	12	B	27	C			52	**30**
13	C	28	D					13	B	28	B				
14	D	29	D					14	C	29	C				
15	D	30	A					15	B	30	D				

TASC Mathematics Practice Tests
Answers and Explanations

TASC Mathematics Practice Test 1

1) Choice B is correct

$\alpha = 180° - 112° = 68°$

$\beta = 180° - 135° = 45°$

$x + \alpha + \beta = 180° \rightarrow x = 180° - 68° - 45° = 67°$

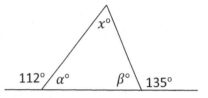

2) Choice A is correct

Simplify and combine like terms.

$(8x^3 - 8x^2 + 2x^4) - (4x^2 - 2x^4 + 2x^3) \Rightarrow (8x^3 - 8x^2 + 2x^4) - 4x^2 + 2x^4 - 2x^3 \Rightarrow$

$4x^4 + 6x^3 - 12x^2$

3) Choice C is correct

The population is increased by 15% and 20%. 15% increase changes the population to 115% of original population. For the second increase, multiply the result by 120%.

$(1.15) \times (1.20) = 1.38 = 138\%$. 38 percent of the population is increased after two years.

4) Choice D is correct

Solve for x.

$-2 \le 2x - 4 < 8 \Rightarrow$ (add 4 all sides) $-2 + 4 \le 2x - 4 + 4 < 8 + 4 \Rightarrow 2 \le 2x < 12 \Rightarrow$ (divide all sides by 2) $1 \le x < 6$, x is between 1 and 6. Choice D represent this inequality.

5) Choice D is correct

$Volume\ of\ a\ box = length \times width \times height = 4 \times 5 \times 6 = 120$

6) Choice C is correct

To find the number of possible outfit combinations, multiply number of options for each factor: $6 \times 5 \times 4 = 120$

7) Choice A is correct

In the stadium the ratio of home fans to visiting fans in a crowd is $5:7$. Therefore, total number of fans must be divisible by $12: 5 + 7 = 12$.

Let's review the choices:

A. 12,324: $12,324 \div 12 = 1,027$

B. 42,326 $42,326 \div 12 = 3,527.166$

C. 44,566 $44,566 \div 12 = 3,713.833$

D. 66,812 $66,812 \div 12 = 5,567.666$

Only choice A when divided by 12 results a whole number.

8) Choice C is correct

Three times of 24,000 is 72,000. One sixth of them cancelled their tickets. One sixth of 72,000 equals 12,000 ($\frac{1}{6} \times 72000 = 12000$). $60,000 (72,000 - 12,000 = 60,000)$ fans are attending this week.

9) Choice A is correct

The area of the square is 595.36. Therefore, the side of the square is square root of the area. $\sqrt{595.36} = 24.4$, Four times the side of the square is the perimeter: $4 \times 24.4 = 97.6$

10) Choice A is correct

$x + 2y = 4$. Plug in the values of x and y from choices provided. Then:

A. $(-4, 4)$ $x + 2y = 4 \rightarrow -4 + 2(4) = 4 \rightarrow -4 + 8 = 4$ This is true!

B. $(1, 2)$ $x + 2y = 4 \rightarrow 1 + 2(2) = 4 \rightarrow 1 + 4 = 4$ This is NOT true!

C. $(-1, 3)$ $x + 2y = 4 \rightarrow -1 + 2(3) = 4 \rightarrow -1 + 6 = 4$ This is NOT true!

D. $(-3, 4)$ $x + 2y = 4 \rightarrow -3 + 2(4) = 4 \rightarrow -3 + 8 = 4$ This is NOT true!

11) Choice A is correct

The width of the rectangle is twice its length. Let x be the length. Then, $width = 2x$

Perimeter of the rectangle is $2\ (width + length) = 2(2x + x) = 60 \Rightarrow 6x = 60 \Rightarrow x = 10$. Length of the rectangle is 10 meters.

12) Choice D is correct

Change the numbers to decimal and then compare.

$\frac{1}{3} = 0.333 \dots , 0.68 , 67\% = 0.67, \frac{4}{5} = 0.80$, Then: $\frac{1}{3} < 67\% < 0.68 < \frac{4}{5}$

13) Choice C is correct

average (mean) $= \frac{\text{sum of terms}}{\text{number of terms}} \Rightarrow 90 = \frac{\text{sum of terms}}{50} \Rightarrow sum = 90 \times 50 = 4500$

The difference of 94 and 69 is 25. Therefore, 25 should be subtracted from the sum.

$4500 - 25 = 4475$, mean $= \frac{\text{sum of terms}}{\text{number of terms}} \Rightarrow$ mean $= \frac{4475}{50} = 89.5$

14) Choice D is correct

For sum of 5: $(1\ \&\ 4)\ and\ (4\ \&\ 1), (2\ \&\ 3)$ and $(3\ \&\ 2)$, therefore we have 4 options.

For sum of 8: $(5\ \&\ 3), (3\ \&\ 5), (4\ \&\ 4)$ and $(2\ \&\ 6)$, and $(6\ \&\ 2)$. we have 5 options. To get a sum of 5 or 8 for two dice: $4 + 5 = 9$
Since, we have $6 \times 6 = 36$ total number of options, the probability of getting a sum of 5 and 8 is 9 out of 36 or $\frac{9}{36} = \frac{1}{4}$.

15) Choice D is correct

Use formula of rectangle prism volume.

$V = (length)(width)(height) \Rightarrow 2000 = (25)(10)(height) \Rightarrow height = 2000 \div 250 = 8$

16) Choice B is correct

The diagonal of the square is 8. Let x be the side.

Use Pythagorean Theorem: $a^2 + b^2 = c^2$

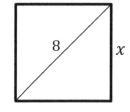

$x^2 + x^2 = 8^2 \Rightarrow 2x^2 = 8^2 \Rightarrow 2x^2 = 64 \Rightarrow x^2 = 32 \Rightarrow x = \sqrt{32}$

The area of the square is: $\sqrt{32} \times \sqrt{32} = 32$

17) Choice B is correct

Probability $= \frac{\text{number of desired outcomes}}{\text{number of total outcomes}} = \frac{18}{12+18+18+24} = \frac{18}{72} = \frac{1}{4}$

18) Choice D is correct

$average = \frac{\text{sum of terms}}{\text{number of terms}} \Rightarrow$ (average of 6 numbers) $12 = \frac{\text{sum of numbers}}{6} \Rightarrow$ sum of 6 numbers is $12 \times 6 = 72$

(average of 4 numbers) $10 = \frac{\text{sum of numbers}}{4} \Rightarrow$ sum of 4 numbers is $10 \times 4 = 40$

$sum\ of\ 6\ numbers - sum\ of\ 4\ numbers = sum\ of\ 2\ numbers\ 72 - 40 = 32$

average of 2 numbers $= \frac{32}{2} = 16$

19) Choice C is correct

Solving Systems of Equations by Elimination

Multiply the first equation by (-2), then add it to the second equation.

$$\begin{array}{r} -2(2x + 5y = 11) \\ 4x - 2y = -26 \end{array} \Rightarrow \begin{array}{r} -4x - 10y = -22 \\ 4x - 2y = -26 \end{array} \Rightarrow -12y = -48 \Rightarrow y = 4$$

Plug in the value of y into one of the equations and solve for x.

$$2x + 5(4) = 11 \Rightarrow 2x + 20 = 11 \Rightarrow 2x = -9 \Rightarrow x = -\frac{9}{2}$$

20) Choice B is correct

The perimeter of the trapezoid is $36 \ cm$. Therefore, the missing side (height) is $= 36 - 8 - 12 - 6 = 10$, Area of a trapezoid: $A = \frac{1}{2} h \ (b_1 + b_2) = \frac{1}{2}(10)(6 + 8) = 70$

21) Choice A is correct

First, find the number. Let x be the number. Write the equation and solve for x.

150% of a number is 75, then: $1.5 \times x = 75 \Rightarrow x = 75 \div 1.5 = 50$

80% of 50 is: $\qquad 0.8 \times 50 = 40$

22) Choice A is correct

Let x be the number of new shoes the team can purchase. Therefore, the team can purchase $160 \ x$. The team had $20,000 and spent $14,000. Now the team can spend on new shoes $6,000 at most. Now, write the inequality: $160x + 14,000 \leq 20,000$

23) Choice B is correct

The probability of choosing a Hearts is $\frac{13}{52} = \frac{1}{4}$

24) Choice D is correct

First, find the sum of five numbers.

$$average = \frac{sum \ of \ terms}{number \ of \ terms} \Rightarrow 26 = \frac{sum \ of \ 5 \ numbers}{5} \Rightarrow sum \ of \ 5 \ numbers = 26 \times 5 = 130.$$

The sum of 5 numbers is 130. If a sixth number that is greater than 42 is added to these numbers, then the sum of 6 numbers must be greater than 162. $130 + 42 = 172$

If the number was 42, then the average of the numbers is: $average = \frac{sum\ of\ terms}{number\ of\ terms} =$ $\frac{172}{6} = 28.66$. Since the number is bigger than 42. Then, the average of six numbers must be greater than 28.66. Choice D is greater than 28.66.

25) Choice C is correct

Let x be the width of the rectangle. Use Pythagorean Theorem: $a^2 + b^2 = c^2$

$x^2 + 5^2 = 13^2 \Rightarrow x^2 + 25 = 169 \Rightarrow x^2 = 169 - 25 = 144 \Rightarrow x = 12$

Area of the rectangle $= length \times width = 5 \times 12 = 60$

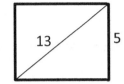

26) Choice C is correct

Th ratio of boy to girls is $4: 7$. Therefore, there are 4 boys out of 11 students. To find the answer, first divide the total number of students by 11, then multiply the result by 4.

$66 \div 11 = 6 \Rightarrow 4 \times 6 = 24$. There are 24 boys and 42 $(66 - 24)$ girls. So, 18 more boys should be enrolled to make the ratio $1: 1$.

27) Choice A is correct

$2,500$ out of $55,000$ equals to $\frac{2500}{55000} = \frac{25}{550} = \frac{1}{22}$

28) Choice D is correct

Jason needs an 77% average to pass for five exams. Therefore, the sum of 5 exams must be at lease $5 \times 77 = 385$, the sum of 4 exams is: $68 + 72 + 85 + 90 = 315$

The minimum score Jason can earn on his fifth and final test to pass is: $385 - 315 = 70$

29) Choice D is correct

Isolate and solve for x.

$\frac{2}{3}x + \frac{1}{6} = \frac{1}{2} \Rightarrow \frac{2}{3}x = \frac{1}{2} - \frac{1}{6} = \frac{1}{3} \Rightarrow \frac{2}{3}x = \frac{1}{3}$

Multiply both sides by the reciprocal of the coefficient of x. $\left(\frac{3}{2}\right)\frac{2}{3}x = \frac{1}{3}\left(\frac{3}{2}\right) \Rightarrow x = \frac{3}{6} = \frac{1}{2}$

30) Choice A is correct

Surface Area of a cylinder $= 2\pi r\ (r + h)$, The radius of the cylinder is $2(4 \div 2)$ inches and its height is 8 inches. Therefore, surface Area of a cylinder $= 2\pi\ (2)(2 + 8) = 40\ \pi$

31) Choice C is correct

The square of a number is $\frac{25}{64}$, then the number is the square root of $\frac{25}{64}$, $\sqrt{\frac{25}{64}} = \frac{5}{8}$, The cube of the number is: $(\frac{5}{8})^3 = \frac{125}{512}$

32) Choice B is correct

Write the numbers in order: $2, 19, 27, 28, 35, 44, 67$

Median is the number in the middle. So, the median is 28.

33) Choice D is correct

Use Pythagorean Theorem: $a^2 + b^2 = c^2, 6^2 + 8^2 = c^2 \Rightarrow 100 = c^2 \Rightarrow c = 10$

34) Choice B is correct

Plug in 104 for F and then solve for C.

$C = \frac{5}{9}(F-32) \Rightarrow C = \frac{5}{9}(104 - 32) \Rightarrow C = \frac{5}{9}(72) = 40$

35) Choice C is correct

Let x be the number. Write the equation and solve for x.

$40\% \ of \ x = 4 \Rightarrow 0.40x = 4 \Rightarrow x = 4 \div 0.40 = 10$

36) Choice D is correct

Let x be all expenses, then $\frac{20}{100}x = \$560 \rightarrow x = \frac{100 \times \$560}{20} = \$2,800$

He spent for his rent: $\frac{27}{100} \times \$2,800 = \$756$

37) Choice C is correct

The distance between Jason and Joe is 15 miles. Jason running at 5.5 miles per hour and Joe is running at the speed of 7 miles per hour. Therefore, every hour the distance is 1.5 miles less. $15 \div 1.5 = 10$

38) Choice D is correct

The failing rate is 11 out of $44 = \frac{11}{44}$, Change the fraction to percent: $\frac{11}{44} \times 100\% = 25\%$

25 percent of students failed. Therefore, 75 percent of students passed the exam.

39) Choice B is correct

Use simple interest formula: $I = prt$

(I = interest, p = principal, r = rate, t = time). $I = (12000)(0.035)(2) = 840$

40) Choice D is correct

Simplify.

$6x^2y^3(2x^2y)^3 = 6x^2y^3(8x^6y^3) = 48x^8y^6$

41) The answer is 20

Use PEMDAS (order of operation):

$[-3 \times (-14) - 48] - (-14) + [3 \times 8] \div 2 = [42 - 48] + 14 + 24 \div 2 = -6 + 14 + 12 = 20$

42) The answer is 2.25

Write a proportion and solve for the missing number. $\frac{32}{12} = \frac{6}{x} \rightarrow 32x = 6 \times 12 = 72, 32x = 72 \rightarrow$ $x = \frac{72}{32} = 2.25$

43) The answer is −27

To solve absolute values equations, write two equations. $2x - 6$ can equal positive 12, or negative 12. Therefore, $2x - 6 = 12 \Rightarrow 2x = 18 \Rightarrow x = 9$

$2x - 6 = -12 \Rightarrow 2x = -12 + 6 = -6 \Rightarrow x = -3$

Find the product of solutions: $-3 \times 9 = -27$

44) The answer is $\frac{1}{3}$

The equation of a line in slope intercept form is: $y = mx + b$

Solve for y. $3x + y = 6 \rightarrow y = -3x + 6$

The slope of this line is -3.

The product of the slopes of two perpendicular lines is -1. Therefore, the slope of a line that is perpendicular to this line is: $m_1 \times m_2 = -1 \Rightarrow -3 \times m_2 = -1 \Rightarrow m_2 = \frac{-1}{-3} = \frac{1}{3}$

45) The answer is 42

Plug in the value of x and y. $3(x - 2y) + (2 - x)^2$ when $x = 5$ and $y = -3$

$3(x - 2y) + (2 - x)^2 = 3(5 - 2(-3)) + (2 - 5)^2 = 3(5 + 6) + (-3)^2 = 33 + 9 = 42$

46) The answer is 175

$-60 = 115 - x$, First, subtract 115 from both sides of the equation. Then: $-60 - 115 = 115 - 115 - x \rightarrow -175 = -x$, Multiply both sides by (-1): $\rightarrow x = 175$

47) The answer is 6

Let y be the width of the rectangle. Then; $15 \times y = 90 \rightarrow y = \frac{90}{15} = 6$

48) The answer is 15

$4x - 1 = 9 \rightarrow 4x = 9 + 1 = 10 \rightarrow x = \frac{10}{4} = 2.5$, Then, $2x + 10 = 2(2.5) + 10 = 5 + 10 = 15$

49) The answer is 63.84

$Average = \frac{sum\ of\ terms}{number\ of\ terms}$. The sum of the weight of all girls is: $18 \times 60 = 1080\ kg$, The sum of the weight of all boys is: $32 \times 66 = 2112\ kg$, The sum of the weight of all students is: $1080 + 2112 = 3192\ kg$

$$Average = \frac{3192}{50} = 63.84$$

50) The answer is 729

If the length of the box is 27, then the width of the box is one third of it, 9, and the height of the box is 3 (one third of the width). The volume of the box is:

$$V = lwh = (27)\,(9)\,(3) = 729$$

51) The answer is 30

Number of males in classroom is: $60 - 42 = 18$

Then, the percentage of males in the classroom is: $\frac{18}{60} \times 100 = 0.3 \times 100 = 30\%$

52) The answer is 35

Let x be the number. Write the equation and solve for x.

$\frac{2}{3} \times 21 = \frac{2}{5}x \rightarrow \frac{2 \times 21}{3} = \frac{2x}{5}$, use cross multiplication to solve for x.

$5 \times 42 = 2x \times 3 \Rightarrow 210 = 6x \Rightarrow x = 35$

TASC Mathematics Practice Test 2

1) Choice D is correct

Write the equation and solve for B: $0.90A = 0.30\,B$, divide both sides by 0.30, then:

$\frac{0.90}{0.30}A = B$, therefore: $B = 3A$, and B is 3 times of A or it's 300% of A.

2) Choice D is correct

To find the number of possible outfit combinations, multiply number of options for each factor: $5 \times 4 \times 7 = 140$

3) Choice C is correct

Use simple interest formula: $I = prt$ ($I = interest, p = principal, r = rate, t = time$)

$I = (12,000)(0.085)(5) = 5,100$

4) Choices B is correct

Some of prime numbers are: $2, 3, 5, 7, 11, 13$. Find the product of two consecutive prime numbers: $2 \times 3 = 6$ (bingo!), $3 \times 5 = 15$ (not in the options), $5 \times 7 = 35$ (not in the options), $7 \times 11 = 77$ (not in the options)

5) Choice C is correct

Let's compare each fraction: $\frac{2}{7} < \frac{3}{8} < \frac{7}{11} < \frac{3}{4}$, Only choice C provides the right order.

6) Choice D is correct

$5^5 = 5 \times 5 \times 5 \times 5 \times 5 = 3,125$

7) Choice C is correct

$$x = \frac{15}{25} = 0.6 = 60\%$$

8) Choice C is correct

Let x be the number. Write the equation and solve for x.

$\frac{2}{3} \times 18 = \frac{2}{5} \ x \Rightarrow \frac{2 \times 18}{3} = \frac{2x}{5}$, use cross multiplication to solve for x.

$5 \times 36 = 2x \times 3 \Rightarrow 180 = 6x \Rightarrow x = 30$

9) Choice C is correct

Use this formula: Percent of Change: $\dfrac{\text{New Value} - \text{Old Value}}{Old\ Value} \times 100\%$

$\dfrac{28,000 - 18,200}{28,000} \times 100\% = -35\%$. The negative sign means that the price decreased

10) Choice D is correct

If the length of the box is 24, then the width of the box is one third of it, 8, and the height of the box is 4 (half of the width). The volume of the box is: $V = lwh = (24)(8)(4) = 768$

11) Choice B is correct

To find the discount, multiply the number by $(100\% - rate\ of\ discount)$.

Therefore, for the first discount we get: $(D)(100\% - 25\%) = (D)(0.75) = 0.75\ D$

For increase of 20%: $(0.75D)(100\% + 20\%) = (0.75\ D)(1.20) = 0.90\ D = 90\%\ of\ D$

12) Choice B is correct

Use the formula for Percent of Change: $\dfrac{\text{New Value} - \text{Old Value}}{Old\ Value} \times 100\%$

$\frac{38-50}{50} \times 100\% = \frac{-12}{50} \times 100\% = -24\%$ (negative sign here means that the new price is less than old price).

13) Choice B is correct

Use the information provided in the question to draw the shape.

Use Pythagorean Theorem: $a^2 + b^2 = c^2$

$90^2 + 120^2 = c^2 \Rightarrow 8,100 + 14,400 = c^2 \Rightarrow 22,500 = c^2 \Rightarrow c = 150$

120 miles

90 miles

14) Choice C is correct

The ratio of boy to girls is 4: 7. Therefore, there are 4 boys out of 11 students. To find the answer, first divide the total number of students by 11, then multiply the result by 4.

$77 \div 11 = 7 \Rightarrow 4 \times 7 = 28$. There are 28 boys and 49 (77 − 28) girls. So, 21 more boys should be enrolled to make the ratio 1: 1

15) Choice B is correct

The question is this: 250.50 is what percent of 300?

Use percent formula: $part = \frac{percent}{100} \times whole$

$250.50 = \frac{percent}{100} \times 300 \Rightarrow 250.50 = \frac{percent \times 300}{100} \Rightarrow 25050 = percent \times 300 \Rightarrow$

$percent = \frac{25050}{300} = 83.5$

250.50 is 83.5% of 300. Therefore, the discount is: $100\% - 83.5\% = 16.50\%$

16) Choice C is correct

If the score of Mia was 80, therefore the score of Ava is 40. Since, the score of Emma was half as that of Ava, therefore, the score of Emma is 20.

17) Choice D is correct

If 19 balls are removed from the bag at random, there will be one ball in the bag. The probability of choosing a brown ball is 1 out of 20. Therefore, the probability of not choosing a brown ball is 19 out of 20 and the probability of having not a brown ball after removing 19 balls is the same.

18) Choice C is correct

The area of the floor is: $8 \, cm \times 32 \, cm = 256 \, cm^2$, The number of tiles needed $= 256 \div 8 = 32$

19) Choice B is correct

The weight of 14.4 meters of this rope is: $14.4 \times 800 \, g = 11,520 \, g$

$1 \, kg = 1000 \, g$, therefore, $11,520 \, g \div 1000 = 11.52 \, kg$

20) Choice C is correct

Let x be the number. Write the equation and solve for x. $(18 - x) \div x = 5$, Multiply both sides by x: $(18 - x) = 5x$, Then add x both sides: $18 = 6x$, now divide both sides by 6: $x = 3$

21) Choice A is correct

The sum of supplement angles is 180. Let x be that angle. Therefore, $x + 4x = 180$

$5x = 180$, divide both sides by 5: $x = 36$

22) Choice C is correct

The average speed of john is: $160 \div 4 = 40$, The average speed of Alice is: $210 \div 3 = 70$,

Write the ratio and simplify. $40 : 70 \Rightarrow 4 : 7$

23) Choice A is correct

Let x be the width of the rectangle. Use Pythagorean Theorem: $a^2 + b^2 = c^2$

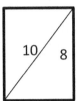

$x^2 + 8^2 = 10^2 \Rightarrow x^2 + 64 = 100 \Rightarrow x^2 = 100 - 64 = 36 \Rightarrow x = 6$

Perimeter of the rectangle $= 2\,(length\ +\ width) = 2\,(8 + 6) = 2\,(14) = 28$

24) Choice B is correct

Let x be the smallest number. Then, these are the numbers:

$x, x + 1, x + 2, x + 3, x + 4$

average $= \dfrac{\text{sum of terms}}{\text{number of terms}} \Rightarrow 38 = \dfrac{x+(x+1)+(x+2)+(x+3)+(x+4)}{5} \Rightarrow 38 = \dfrac{5x+10}{5} \Rightarrow$

$190 = 5x + 10 \Rightarrow 180 = 5x \Rightarrow x = 36$

25) Choice C is correct

$average = \dfrac{sum\ of\ terms}{number\ of\ terms} = \dfrac{12+10+4+8+11+9}{6} = \dfrac{54}{6} = 9$

26) Choice B is correct

$average = \dfrac{sum\ of\ terms}{number\ of\ terms}$

The sum of the weight of all girls is: $20 \times 58 = 1,160\ kg$, The sum of the weight of all boys is: $30 \times 66 = 1,980\ kg$, The sum of the weight of all students is: $1,160 + 1,980 = 3,140\ kg$. $average = \dfrac{3,140}{50} = 62.8$

27) Choice C is correct

Let x be the original price.

If the price of a laptop is decreased by 20% to \$420, then: $80\%\ of\ x = 420 \Rightarrow 0.80x = 420 \Rightarrow x = 420 \div 0.80 = 525$

28) Choice B is correct

Write the numbers in order: $5, 6, 9, 10, 14, 16, 19$. Since we have 7 numbers (7 is odd), then the median is the number in the middle, which is 10.

29) Choice C is correct

$\$9 \times 10 = \$90$,   Petrol use: $10 \times 2 = 20$ liters

Petrol cost: $20 \times \$1 = \$20$, Money earned: $\$90 - \$20 = \$70$

30) Choice D is correct

Surface Area of a cylinder $= 2\pi r \, (r + h)$,

The radius of the cylinder is 8 inches and its height is 12 inches. π is 3.14. Then:

Surface Area of a cylinder $= 2 \, (3.14) \, (8) \, (8 + 16) = 1,205.76$

31) Choice C is correct

Use distance formula: $Distance = Rate \times time \Rightarrow 390 = 60 \times T$, divide both sides by 60: $\frac{390}{60} = T \Rightarrow T = 6.5 \, hours$. Change hours to minutes for the decimal part. $0.5 \, hours = 0.5 \times 60 = 30 \, minutes$

32) Choice D is correct

The equation of a line is in the form of $y = mx + b$, where m is the slope of the line and b is the $y - intercept$ of the line. Two points $(1, 2)$ and $(-1, 6)$ are on line A. Therefore, the slope of the line A is: $slope \; of \; line \; A = \frac{y_2 - y_1}{x_2 - x_1} = \frac{6-2}{-1-1} = \frac{4}{-2} = -2$

The slope of line A is -2. Thus, the formula of the line A is: $y = mx + b = -2x + b$, choose a point and plug in the values of x and y in the equation to solve for b. Let's choose point $(1, 2)$. Then: $y = -2x + b \rightarrow 2 = -2(1) + b \rightarrow b = 2 + 2 = 4$. The equation of line A is: $y = -2x + 4$

Now, let's review the choices provided:

A. $(-1, 2)$ $y = -2x + 4 \rightarrow 2 = -2(-1) + 4 = 6$ This is not true.

B. $(5, 7)$ $y = -2x + 4 \rightarrow 7 = -2(5) + 4 = -6$ This is not true.

C. $(3, 4)$ $y = -2x + 4 \rightarrow 4 = -2(3) + 4 = -2$ This is not true.

D. $(3, -2)$ $y = -2x + 4 \rightarrow -2 = -2(3) + 4 = -2$ This is true!

33) Choice A is correct

Let x be the number of years. Therefore, $\$2,000$ per year equals $2000x$. starting from $\$23,000$ annual salary means you should add that amount to $2000x$. Income more than that is: $I > 2000x + 23000$

34) Choice C is correct

Let x be the original price. If the price of the sofa is decreased by 18% to $\$451$, then: $82\% \; of \; x = 451 \Rightarrow 0.82x = 451 \Rightarrow x = 451 \div 0.82 = 550$

35) Choice D is correct

Use Pythagorean Theorem: $a^2 + b^2 = c^2$

$3^2 + 4^2 = c^2 \Rightarrow 9 + 16 = c^2 \Rightarrow 25 = c^2 \Rightarrow c = 5$

36) Choice B is correct

The percent of girls playing tennis is: $50\% \times 30\% = 0.50 \times 0.30 = 0.15 = 15\%$

37) Choice C is correct

Add the first 5 numbers. $40 + 45 + 50 + 35 + 55 = 225$

To find the distance traveled in the next 5 hours, multiply the average by number of hours.

$Distance = Average \times Rate = 75 \times 5 = 375$

Add both numbers. $375 + 225 = 600$

38) Choice A is correct

Area of the circle is less than 16π. Use the formula of areas of circles.

$Area = \pi r^2 \Rightarrow 64\pi > \pi r^2 \Rightarrow 64 > r^2 \Rightarrow r < 8$

Radius of the circle is less than 8. Let's put 8 for the radius. Now, use the circumference formula:
$Circumference = 2\pi r = 2\pi\,(8) = 16\pi$

Since the radius of the circle is less than 8. Then, the circumference of the circle must be less than 16π. Only choice A is less than 16π.

39) Choice C is correct

$\begin{cases} x + 4y = 10 \\ 5x + 5y = 20 \end{cases} \rightarrow$ Multiply the top equation by -5 then,

$\begin{cases} -5x - 20y = -50 \\ \quad 5x + 5y = 20 \end{cases} \rightarrow$ Add two equations

$-15y = -30 \rightarrow y = 2$, plug in the value of y into the first equation

$x + 4y = 10 \rightarrow x + 4(2) = 10 \rightarrow x + 8 = 10$. Subtract 12 from both sides of the equation. Then: $x + 8 = 10 \rightarrow x = 2$

40) Choice C is correct

6% of the volume of the solution is alcohol. Let x be the volume of the solution.

Then: 6% of $x = 42$ $ml \Rightarrow 0.06x = 42 \Rightarrow x = 42 \div 0.06 = 700$

41) The answer is 38

Use PEMDAS (order of operation): $32 - 3 \times (6) - [8 + 16 \times (-5)] \div 2 - 12 = 32 - 3 \times (6) - (-72) \div 2 - 12 = 32 - 18 - (-72) \div 2 - 12 = 32 - 18 - (-36) - 12 = 32 - 18 + 36 - 12 = 38$

42) The answer is 32

First draw an isosceles triangle. Remember that two sides of the triangle are equal.

Let put a for the legs. Then:

Isosceles right triangle

$a = 8 \Rightarrow$ area of the triangle is $= \frac{1}{2}(8 \times 8) = \frac{64}{2} = 32$

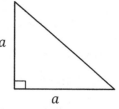

43) The answer is 38

$\text{average} = \frac{\text{sum of terms}}{\text{number of terms}} \Rightarrow 20 = \frac{11+13+18+x}{4} \Rightarrow 80 = 42 + x \Rightarrow x = 38$

44) The answer is 264

The perimeter of the trapezoid is 62.

Therefore, the missing side (height) is $= 62 - 16 - 10 - 12 = 24$

Area of a trapezoid: $A = \frac{1}{2}h\,(b_1 + b_2) = \frac{1}{2}(24)(10 + 12) = \frac{1}{2}(24)(22) = \frac{1}{2} \times 528 = 264$

45) The answer is 110

$\frac{2.75}{2.50} = 110$

46) The answer is 1.25

$2x - 6 = 6.5 \rightarrow 2x = 6.5 + 6 \rightarrow 2x = 12.5 \rightarrow x = \frac{12.5}{2} = 6.25$

Then: $-3x + 20 = -3(6.25) + 20 = -18.75 + 20 = 1.25$

47) The answer is 25

The percent of girls take drawing class is: $75\% \times \frac{1}{3} = 25\%$.

48) The answer is 52

Since $N = 8$, substitute 8 for N in the equation $\frac{x-4}{6} = N$, which gives $\frac{x-4}{6} = 8$. Multiplying both sides of $\frac{x-4}{6} = 8$ by 6 gives $x - 4 = 48$ and then adding 4 to both sides of $x - 4 = 48$, then: $x = 52$.

49) The answer is 18

The question is this: 529.72 is what percent of 646? Use percent formula:

$part = \frac{percent}{100} \times whole.$ $529.72 = \frac{percent}{100} \times 646 \Rightarrow 529.72 = \frac{percent \times 646}{100} \Rightarrow$

$52972 = percent \times 646 \Rightarrow percent = \frac{52972}{646} = 82$

529.72 is 82% of 646. Therefore, the discount is: $100\% - 82\% = 18\%$

50) The answer is 0

The input value is -2. Then: $x = -2$, $f(x) = 2(-2)^2 + 4(-2) = 2(4) - 8 = 8 - 8 = 0$

51) The answer is $\frac{1}{15}$ or 0.06

Write the ratio of $5a$ to $2b$. $\frac{5a}{2b} = \frac{1}{6}$

Use cross multiplication and then simplify. $5a \times 6 = 2b \times 1 \rightarrow 30a = 2b \rightarrow a = \frac{2b}{30} = \frac{b}{15}$

Now, find the ratio of a to b. $\frac{a}{b} = \frac{\frac{b}{15}}{b} \rightarrow \frac{b}{15} \div b = \frac{b}{15} \times \frac{1}{b} = \frac{b}{15b} = \frac{1}{15} = 0.06$

52) The answer is 30

The rate of construction company$= \frac{40 \text{ cm}}{1 \text{ min}} = 40 \frac{cm}{min}$

Height of the wall after 50 minutes $= \frac{40 \text{ cm}}{1 \text{ min}} \times 50 \text{ min} = 2{,}000 cm$

Let x be the height of wall, then $\frac{2}{3}x = 2{,}000 cm \rightarrow x = \frac{3 \times 2{,}000}{2} \rightarrow x = 3{,}000 \text{ cm} = 30 \ m$

"Effortless Math Education" Publications

Effortless Math authors' team strives to prepare and publish the best quality TASC Mathematics learning resources to make learning Math easier for all. We hope that our publications help you learn Math in an effective way and prepare for the TASC test.

We all in Effortless Math wish you good luck and successful studies!

Effortless Math Authors

www.EffortlessMath.com

... So Much More Online!

✓ FREE Math lessons

✓ More Math learning books!

✓ Mathematics Worksheets

✓ Online Math Tutors

Need a PDF version of this book?

Visit www.EffortlessMath.com

Made in the USA
Middletown, DE
28 January 2020